ARMIES AND ENEMIES OF LOUIS XIV

Volume 1: Western Europe 1688–1714 – France, Great Britain, Holland

Mark Allen

'This is the Century of the Soldier', Falvio Testir, Poet, 1641

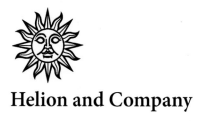

Helion and Company

Helion and Company Limited
Unit 8 Amherst Business Centre
Budbrooke Road
Warwick
CV34 5WE
England
Tel. 01926 499 619
Fax 0121 711 4075
Email: info@helion.co.uk
Website: www.helion.co.uk
Twitter: @helionbooks
Visit our blog at http://blog.helion.co.uk/

Published by Helion and Company 2018
Designed and typeset by Serena Jones
Cover designed by Paul Hewitt, Battlefield Design (www.battlefield-design.co.uk)
Printed by Henry Ling Limited, Dorchester, Dorset

ISBN 978-1-911628-05-7

British Library Cataloguing-in-Publication Data.
A catalogue record for this book is available from the British Library.

For details of other military history titles published by Helion and Company
Limited, contact the above address, or visit our website: http://www.helion.co.uk

We always welcome receiving book proposals from prospective authors.

For Lily

Contents

Foreword

When Duncan McFarlane, the perspicacious proprietor of *Wargames Illustrated* commissioned Mark Allen to write a series of articles beginning with a four parter on The War of the Grand Alliance followed by another twenty odd feature pieces, it was as if the rains had finally come after almost perpetual drought. Since that issue of the magazine way back in 1990 the rain has continued to fall softly but steadily from a variety of sources but it was Mark who very definitely seeded the clouds.

For enthusiasts keen to understand the armies, uniforms and flags of the period 1660–1714 the activity is akin to peering through an old-style window frosted with ice. Much is ill-defined and a deal of energy is required to clear meagre patches through which to view. For the want of information, researchers past and present predicate general assumptions on tiny fragments of data mined from scattered and obscure original sources. Such extrapolative activities centred on dress conventions, weapons and tactics can steer the less enquiring mind toward lazy conclusions which often become accepted wisdom whether true or not. The small community of dedicated researchers responsible for bringing data to a wider readership has occasionally adopted a defensive posture if its deductions are challenged. Mark has never been precious about his work despite putting a great deal of time and effort into its compilation. His policy of active self-critique and exchange of data with others has created a clearer understanding for all. His wholesale reworking of previously published material relating to the Thirty Years War is testimony to his self-critical approach.

Mark Allen's pieces have served as a continual go-to source for those new to the period and hungry for a start point as well as seasoned students who continually cross-refer and calibrate their own discoveries. Building on the excellent work by Alan Sapherson, Stephen Ede-Borrett, Pat Condray and others, he offered succinct text supported by original and engaging illustrations.

It is my great privilege to introduce material which has finally been combined into a hard copy volume. This content inspired and sustained my own passion for a period often described as the cradle of modern national armies. The plates and text herein are an essential for anyone serious about the study of 17th and early 18th century military history. Mark Allen's work, in particular the meticulously posed battle shots accompanying the first four articles, combined with Duncan's beautiful photography, inspired many of us to paint and convert in imitation.

Thankfully, this long neglected period is now supported by various figure ranges, rule systems, scenarios and websites and that is due in no small measure to the content of this long overdue book.

Barry Hilton
April 2018

Introduction

This book had its origins in a series of magazine articles that appeared in *Wargames Illustrated* under the stewardship of Duncan Macfarlane, from 1990 until 2003. My interest in this period was spurred by a number of re-enactment events, planned to coincide with the 300th anniversary of Monmouth's Rebellion and the availability of the Dixon range of 25mm figures, brilliantly and innovatively designed by Mark Copplestone.

My attempts to find the necessary information to enable me to paint these creations proved difficult, so I embarked on a period of research to 'fill in' the gaps in my knowledge. It might be useful to state here, that this book is more of a case of pulling together threads from reliable secondary sources, than revolutionary new discoveries gleaned from poring over musty tomes or IT files in libraries or catacombs!

Since the original publication of this material, much has happened including the arrival of the excellent publications by the Pike and Shot Society, the work of Robert Hall, and his confederates. Additionally my friend Steve Ede-Borrett has continued his research with items in the Pike and Shot magazine *Arquebusier* and culminating in his new book on James II's Army, for which I was pleased to be able contribute the plates and which was a revisit and revision of his excellent 1980s publication for Raider Games.

It wasn't possible to undergo a total revision of this material, in the light of this new research, or indeed to add chapters on the areas that weren't covered before, French cavalry, dragoons and artillery, and the same with the British, but I hope to be able to deal with this in a second volume.

Finally a chance to thank those without whom this book would not be appearing and whose efforts and support started me down this road, thirty or more years ago: Charles Singleton, my friend and editor at Helion, Duncan McFarlane, Mark Copplestone, Steve Ede-Borrett, and Barry Hilton and Phil Olley, for an inspirational coming together in Birmingham in 1995, which probably led to the original series being extended long past its 'sell by date'.

My thanks also to Paul Hewitt for his work on restoring the plates and to Serena Jones for her editorial and layout work.

Mark Allen
Redditch 2018

1

The War of the Grand Alliance

Part 1: 1688–1697

Introduction

The War of the Grand Alliance, or the League of Augsburg, or the Nine Years' War as it was alternatively known, was the final great confrontation between the old enemies, Louis XIV and William III of Orange. William had, throughout his life, opposed the expansionist policies of the French in the Spanish Netherlands which threatened the security of Holland. Indeed he had had to face a full-scale invasion in 1672 which led to further French gains in lands and strategically important fortresses in the treaty that followed.

In 1688 events changed dramatically when a group of English Protestants, worried by the increasing autocracy of Catholic King James II, invited William to England to 'Defend the Protestant Religion' and also the rights of his wife Mary, daughter of James in the succession to the English throne. After a short, almost bloodless campaign William was King of England and James in enforced exile in France.

During the 'Revolution' of 1688 Ireland had remained largely loyal to King James. His appointed deputy, Richard Talbot, Earl of Tyrconnell had succeeded in replacing the Protestant officers in the army with Catholics, so that when in 1688 the army in England was unable to respond to the Williamite invasion due to divisions and disloyalty the same could not be said of King James's Irish arrny. Therefore when James, spurred on by his cousin Louis, sought to regain his kingdom, Ireland was the chosen place to begin the reconquest.

William was now facing a war on two fronts, in Ireland and, more importantly, as he saw it, in Flanders against the French. There were however some allies in this unequal struggle against the might of Louis XIV.

Before the invasion of England an agreement had been made with Denmark and Brandenburg-Prussia to supply troops to defend the Dutch border, and both the Austrian Empire and Bavaria joined the alliance and signed the treaty of the 'League of Augsburg', agreeing to commit soldiers and money to the anti-Louis crusade.

So the army that went to face the Jacobites in Ireland was very much an 'international' force. As well as English and Scots troops, both new recruits and old soldiers of the 'pre-revolution' army, there were Dutch troops from William's own army and three regiments of French Huguenot infantry, as well as a brigade of Danish mercenaries, who made up nearly one third of the army.

This chapter does not intend to look in detail at the campaign in Ireland or the later events in Flanders, but to concentrate for the moment on the tactics and drills of the many armies involved between 1688 and 1697.

The War of the Grand Alliance was a period of evolution in Warfare. It was, in many ways, the last great seventeenth century war, the last pike and shot engagement, but already signs were showing of what the next century would herald.

The nations involved varied enormously in their development of new weaponry and tactical doctrines. Few were as forward as the Danes who, by the time of the Boyne (1690), had completely re-equipped their troops with flintlock weapons, nor as backward as the 'armed might', of Hessen-Kassel who only discarded their obsolete matchlocks at the beginning of the Spanish Succession war (1702). Most armies fell somewhere between the two extremes with their standard infantry regiments being equipped with a mixture of matchlocks and flintlocks and the only units armed solely with the latter being those who had an artillery aspect to their use, like the French Fusiliers du Roi.

The other weapon which was to disappear before 1702 was the 'noble puissant' pike. The number of pikes which a battalion of foot might deploy had declined throughout the century until by 1690 most units had only one fifth of their men using the pike. The pike, in the hands of the great mercenary soldiers of the previous century had been a weapon of attack, but the improvements in firepower in later years made columns of pikemen a tempting target for musketeers. After 1660 the numbers of pikemen in most European armies had dropped to the point where they had little or no offensive tactical use. This heralded the major change in the tactical use of infantry, no longer could an army's pike force be relied upon to break the opposing foot, instead the reliance had to be placed on firepower.

The delivery of firepower became, therefore the subject which most great military minds turned to in the last quarter of the seventeenth century.

Major Events of the War of the Grand Alliance 1688–1697

1686
Formation of the 'League of Augsburg', an anti-French coalition between Austria, Sweden, Spain, Holland, and the Protestant Princes of Northern Germany.

1688
Williamite invasion of England. French seizure of the Palatinate.

1689
Formation of the 'Grand Alliance' between England, Austria, Holland, Bavaria, Brandenburg, Spain, Savoy, Saxony and Hanover.

Catholics under the Duke of Schomberg besiege Williamite army lands in Ireland, but fail to capture Derry and Enniskillen. In Flanders the Prince of Waldeck and John Churchill (later Duke of Marlborough) defeat the French under the Duc d'Humieres at Walcourt. In Scotland James Graham of Claverhouse raises the Jacobite clans and defeats government forces at Killiekrankie. Claverhouse is killed in the battle.

1690
Battle of Fleurus: the Marechal Duc Jean d'Luxembourg (replacing d'Humieres) defeats Waldeck. Battle of the Boyne, William defeats Jacobite army; James returns to France. Battle of Saffarda: French forces defeat Savoyards. Having failed to capture Dunkeld the previous year the Jacobite army in Scotland is surprised and destroyed at Cromdale.

1691
Luxembourg takes Mons and Hal. Battle of Aughrim: Williamite army under Dutch general Ginkel defeats Jacobites commanded by French general St. Ruth. This is the end of the last Catholic field army and the rest of the war consists of besieging the last Jacobite-held towns.

1692
Siege and capture of Namur by the French. Battle of Steenkirk, attempt by William to surprise Luxembourg's encampment results in a serious defeat for the allies.

1693
Battle of Neerwinden or Landen: major defeat for William at the hands of the Duc de Luxembourg. Battle of Marsaglia: Duke of Savoy is again soundly defeated by the French under Marechal Catinat. French take Charleroi.

1695
Death of the Duc de Luxembourg, succeeded by Marechal de Villeroi. William recaptures Namur.

1696
General Talmash's attack on Brest, with an English force, fails. Savoy makes peace with France.

1697
September/October, Treaty of Ryswick. Peace treaty is concluded with a return to the 1679 borders.

Part 2: The Army of Louis XIV

The decline of the number of pikemen in a unit had made the firearm the decisive factor in determining the outcome of infantry combat. No longer could polearms be relied upon to deliver the *coup de grâce* in the melee and therefore the methods used to deliver fire upon the enemy became a critical element in the pursuit of military success. Basically two tactical doctrines existed:

Firing by Ranks

The musketeers in the armies of the Thirty Years' War had deployed six to eight ranks deep and fired one rank at a time, whilst the other ranks were reloading. Two methods were employed to use this technique, one called 'introduction' to advance firing, and another called 'extroduction', used to retire firing. In the latter case the rank which had just fired would retire to the rear, and begin to reload, while the new front rank gave fire, in the former the rank which had just fired stood where it was to reload, and the rear rank marched to the front of the unit, and gave fire. The Swedes introduced 'volley' fire into the equation by allowing several ranks to 'hold their fire' and give a volley at the same time. This enabled a decisive blow to be delivered, but left the majority of the unit unloaded should a surprise attack follow. This became the technique used, by most nations, in the late seventeenth century to deliver infantry fire on an enemy.

Platoon Firing

The big problem therefore was fire control. Platoon firing solved most of this problem and became the basis for all infantry firing for the next hundred years. How did it work?

In essence the firing line was organised into numbered platoons who fired in succession. The fire normally began with the two platoons at the ends of the line and worked inwards, but many countries evolved their own methods as they adopted the system. Firing small parts of a unit in succession gave a continuous fire yet left a considerable portion of a unit's strength loaded and ready should an emergency occur.

The Dutch had developed the system and in 1688 its use was limited to them and their allies. The tragedy for the Alliance was that they had to wait 16 years to find a general capable of exploiting this tactical superiority.

Part 3: The Tactics of Mounted Troops

Duncan Macfarlane advanced a theory that the adoption of the charge at the gallop was dependant on the quality of horseflesh available at the time. Whether this is the correct reason or not it is undoubtably true that throughout history the tactics used by cavalry forces have involved the rediscovery of the value of 'cold steel' tactics in between periods of static or missile-based theories.

In the seventeenth century this again was the case, the early years of the Thirty Years' War were dominated by heavy armoured cuirassier cavalry, the direct descendents of the German 'reiters' of the previous century, performing the relatively static 'caracole' tactic.

The Caracole

It sounds like a dance and in many respects it resembled one. Dense bodies of horse, sometimes only as wide as half a troop and dozens of ranks deep would close with their enemy to 'point blank' range and then proceed to fire each pistol-armed rank in turn, those who had already fired returning to the rear to reload, ready to fire again when their turn came. With the advantages of hindsight it is easy to see the problems associated with this system, and how it would be so easily overthrown by a more aggressive opponent. But why had the tactic been adopted in the first place?

Caracoling had originally been introduced to combat the lance-armed gendarme, whose wild charges delivered at the gallop in a single rank could be broken by the disciplined firepower and depth of formation of the German pistoleers hired by their opponents. It was for this reason that, when western European nations later readopted the charge, the Imperialists and others who faced the Turkish cavalry, using similar tactics to sixteenth century gendarmes, retained firepower-based approaches. By the late seventeenth century the tactic had evolved. Chandler states that by the time of the War of the Grand Alliance the French cavalry 'still advanced at the trot to fire, but this it now gave in three ranks all at once. Following the discharge of pistol and carbine, the squadrons spurred through the smoke to engage in melee, swords in hand. There was, however, relatively little attempt to press home the attack with the ruthless vigour of a Gustavus or a Cromwell.'

The Charge

Reintroduced by the aforementioned Gustavus Adolphus, King of Sweden into the Thirty Years' War, the cavalry charge became again, for a while, the dominant tactic in western European cavalry combat. Most nations readopted a version of it, some introducing a pistol firing element which delivered little fire and lost most of the momentum of the charge, so that by the time of the War of the Grand Alliance only the Swedes, whose involvement was minimal, still continued with the charge at the gallop. Until reading the book by Brent Nosworthy, I was of the opinion that the French had introduced firepower tactics shortly after the end of the Thirty Years' War and therefore received their due 'come-uppance' when Marlborough's disciplined cavalry charges, delivered at 'a good round trot' destroyed their reputation during the War of Spanish Succession. However, Nosworthy offers compelling arguments for the quite late readoption of firepower tactics by Louis' armies and goes as far as to say that it was not until the early years of the eighteenth century that the reintroduction was complete. Nosworthy implies that French cavalry regiments had no single body of regulations to follow, so it is likely that individual regiments deployed in whatever way the colonel thought fit. The chronological development according to Nosworthy was, 'that French cavalry upon occasions were using the caracole as late as 1672. After this date, the French cavalry developed a more aggressive quality, and enjoyed their great successes when they attacked at speed, sword in hand. Though these charges were furious, little attention was paid to the order of the formation after the horses were made to advance at a fast trot'. He goes on to explain that the admiration felt, by some element of the French military for the 'German' method of receiving an attack, i.e. receiving charges at the halt and using small arms fire to break up the enemy before counter-attacking, caused a major rethink during the final years of the century.

French Cavalry

French cavalry consisted of three separate bodies, which were:

The Maison du Roi

The Gendarmerie de France

The Cavalerie Legere

Maison du Roi

This was, as its name implies, the royal guard of the king of France. Its mounted arm consisted of:

Gendarmes de la *Garde* (one company of 200 men)

Chevauxleger de la *Garde* (one company of 200 men)

Garde du Corps (four companies of 400 men)

Mousquetaires (two companies of 250 men)

Grenadiers a Cheval (one company of 250 men)

Gendarmerie de France

An elite formation of 16 companies whose strength according to Rene Chartrand varied between 80 and 200 men. Some of the companies were called chevauxleger, but they dressed and performed as gendarmes.

Cavalerie Legere

Not light horse in any sense, but used as a term to difference them from the above, this force consisted of the rest of the French battle cavalry.

French Cavalry Organisation

Cavalry regiments consisted of up to 12 companies, formed into four sqaudrons of three companies each. One of these squadrons was, I presume, a depot squadron as on no order of battle can I find more than three squadrons deployed.

The Regiment at War

The number of squadrons which a regiment might field could vary. To illustrate this I have listed below the cavalry regiments fielded by the French at the War of the Spanish Succession battles of Eckeren (30 June 1703) and Spire (15 November 1703). Whilst historically outside the remit of these articles I think it fair to assume that similar mixes of regiments were used in the War of the Grand Alliance.

Part 4: Dress, Equipment, Dragoons

History and Tactics

The origins of the dragoon is a subject of some dispute, but they appear to have evolved in the French army from the bands of mounted arquebusiers who were prevalent in the armies of the religious wars of the sixteenth century. Throughout the seventeenth century they were used as mounted infantry; riding to the battlefield and then dismounting to fight. This combined role left them feeling neither part of the infantry nor the cavalry, and consequently they were unpopular with both. Their unpopularity with the rest of the military was echoed by the populace in general as they earned a reputation during the Thirty Years' War for rapine and pillage, during the foraging expeditions upon which they were sent. In essence they fulfilled the tasks in an army which a hundred years later hussars and light dragoons would attend to. On the battlefields of the early to mid seventeenth century the dragoons of an army would be dismounted and sent to guard strongpoints or to line hedges, etc. only 'mounting-up' to harry the retreating enemy or to flee, depending on the outcome of the engagement.

During the later years of the century some German states began to use their dragoons as a sort of second class cavalry, but the French still persevered with the tactics of the Thirty Years' War. They also seemed to have used dismounted dragoons to lead assaults on fortifications or defended villages and all in all the French dragoon was more highly regarded in the army of Louis XIV than dragoons in other armies. Despite this, when there were shortages of horse flesh the dragoons were the first to suffer, witness Tallard's army at Blenheim where, deployed on foot in the area between the village of Blindheim and the River Danube, were several regiments of dragoons whose horses had died of 'glanders'.

Organisation

Apart from the titles of their officers, which were derived from their infantry background, French Dragoon regiments were organised in exactly the same way as their cavalry, i.e. 12 companies formed into four squadrons of three companies each. Like the cavalry one squadron was, I presume, a depot squadron, as no order of battle lists more than two or three squadrons deployed.

2

The Dutch Army

The Dutch army in general and the infantry in particular, were the backbone of the Grand Alliance's opposition to Louis XIV in Flanders during the Nine Years' War, 1688–97. The Stadtholder Willem III (later King William III of Britain and Ireland) had taken control of his country's army at the height of the French invasion of 1672 and had weathered the storm which seemed likely to overwhelm the Netherlands. He achieved this with a field army of less than 15,000 men. ably aided by the policy of deliberately flooding most of the Dutch lowlands to impede the French advance. He spent the following years enlarging and training a force able to stand up to his aggressive southern neighbour.

The Dutch Infantry in the Nine Years' War

By the time of the Nine Years' War the Dutch infantry was probably 'man-for-man' the finest in Europe, and whilst it did not enjoy a period of consistent success, on the battlefield it showed a durability and a capacity to extricate not only itself but also the rest of the allied army from difficult situations. Time and time again heroic rearguard actions, most notably at Steenkirk and Landen saved the army from complete destruction and although by the end of the war the British infantry was in many ways its equal this was not the case earlier. The Dutch infantry and its commanders were also at the forefront of military thinking, developing both platoon firing and as a consequence, less deep formations, allowing a greater weight of fire to be laid down by a battalion. These advances really came into play during the War of the Spanish Succession when the Dutch and British infantry were able for the first time to gain an ascendency over their French opponents. Much of this was down to the arrival of a commander capable of mastering the French war machine, John Churchill, Duke of Marlborough; but he was assisted greatly by Dutch innovation.

However, to return to the earlier period in question, William III managed to build up the strength of the native Dutch infantry to over 50 regiments, as well as other regiments made up of English, Scots, Swiss, and Swedes. The army's strength was further enhanced by subsidy troops from many of the smaller German states, paid for by either the Dutch States-General or by Britain.

Part One: The Dutch Foot Guards (*Garde te Voet*) of William III

Introduction

In 1688 a third regiment of Foot Guards was added to the establishment of the English army. These were not the famous Scots Guards, who were still part of the Scottish army at this time, but the equally famous 'Blue Guards' of King William III. One of the earliest units raised as part of the armed forces of the Dutch Republic, the *Garde* te line formed the backbone of the Williamite invasion force of 1688, and were, along with a number of other Dutch units, paid for by the British crown during the early years of the Nine Years' War (1688–97).

History and Service

The Netherlands were formed from a number of different provinces which all maintained a degree of autonomy regarding the raising of troops for the army. The Foot Guards were raised and maintained by Holland, the largest province, which provided the bulk of the support for the army. Indeed of the 56 native Dutch infantry regiments in service during some part of William's reign 27 were financed by Holland.[1]

The Guards were always at the forefront of the action, tending to be used as an advance guard, rather than as a tactical reserve in the manner of Napoleon's 'Old Grumblers'. At the Boyne they were first into the river, leading the frontal attack at Oldbridge. Along with the supporting Danish battalions, they suffered greatly from the attacks of the Jacobite horse as they attempted to gain a foothold on the opposite bank. In this attack the Guards suffered 150 casualties out of 1,931 men engaged.

The *Garde te Voet* were also involved in William III's two great Continental battles against the Duke of Luxembourg, at Steenkirk and Neerwinden. At the first of these the British Foot, who bore the brunt of the fighting, blamed the commander of the Blue Guards, Count Henrik van Solms, for the failure of the Dutch to support their attacks on the French encampment. Solms was killed in the defence of the village of Landen during the other defeat of King William's forces at Neerwinden, in 1693. His death was not mourned by the British contingent in the army! He was replaced by Duke Ferdinand Wilhelm von Württemberg-Teck (1659–1701),[2] who in turn was replaced by Prince Walrad von Nassau-Saarbrücken-Ottweiler in 1701.

Organisation

Unlike most Dutch infantry regiments, which were of single battalion strength, the *Garde te Voet* consisted of three battalions. The three battalions were made up of a regimental staff and 26 companies; 24 of the companies contained 89

---

1 The other contributors were as follows: Gelderland five, Friesland eight. Overyssel two, Groningen six, Zealand six, Utrecht seven and Drenthe one (these numbers do not add up to 56, as units were often jointly funded or changed hands during their existence).

2 Ironically Solms was replaced by the man who had command of the advance guard of British infantry that he was believed to have let down, i.e. Württemberg.

corporals and private soldiers, with one captain, one lieutenant, one ensign, two sergeants, two drummers, one clerk and three servants for the officers. The two other companies were the Life company, which numbered 120 in total, including 11 officers, and the Grenadier company,3 which contained two extra officers. The three battalions contained nine companies in the first and second battalions and eight in the third. During this period around one fifth of the guardsmen were pikemen.

Arms and Equipment

The arms and equipment carried by Dutch troops developed from matchlock to flintlock and from apostles to cartouche, as with other western European nations. At the beginning of the period the matchlock was carried by most foot soldiers with the exception of grenadiers, who were armed with a shortened 'snaphance'. The number of flintlocks among musketeers gradually increased, but the matchlock was probably not entirely replaced until after the Peace of Rijswijk (1697). Questions regarding the replacement of outdated equipment amongst Dutch troops are difficult to answer. Visual sources for the period appear to show a distinct look to Dutch infantry, particularly the Guards. This consists of crossed buff leather shoulder belts with the one over the right shoulder being a sword baldric, the other a collar of gunpowder charges. However in none of the images is it clear that the latter belt has any charges, and indeed some modern reconstructions, using these pictures as their source, show a cartridge box with a large nap attached to the end of this shoulder belt. The problem is whether these pictures can be trusted; nearly every one of the many portraits of William III in a 'martial' pose shows the famous river crossing of Blue Guards at the Boyne and all show clearly the crossed belts, but fail to clarify the points regarding charges or cartridge box (see Plate 1, figs. A and B and Plate 3, fig. A, for depiction of carrying cross belts). So far so good, but what if all these illustrations have been taken from one faulty original source? Two possible earlier sources are the works of Romeyn de Hooghe and the painting of William's landing at Torbay in 1688. In the latter picture the *Garde te Voet* can be seen wearing the equipment as noted above, but there is no evidence that this was taken from life and may well have been copied from de Hooghe's political cartoons which applaud the achievements of William of Orange, and which date, in many cases from the mid 1670s. The only other useful visual source is the watercolour in the Royal collection which depicts Dutch, or possibly English troops, and probably dates from the late 1690s: it shows the use of the waistbelt to carry the sword and the shoulder belt for the cartridge box. A serious study of the development of this equipment remains to be done and may never be possible given the limited sources. Unlike the majority of their British allies the Dutch pikemen wore body armour, although dispensing with the helmet and wearing the same felt hat as their musketeer counterparts.

---

3 Most Dutch units of this period did not have an actual Grenadier company, but each 'musketeer' company had Grenadiers on its strength. These were then formed together to perform specific tasks.

Dress

That the Dutch *Garde te Voet* wore blue may be safely assumed, however beyond this further references to the uniform worn enter into the realm of speculation. Most early visual sources show the blue coats 'turned up' in a dirty orange, with breeches and stockings to match, and at the other end of the chronology by the middle of the third decade of the eighteenth century the orange had been replaced by red. Alan Sapherson, whose excellent publication is probably the best published source on William's army, lists only two references for the *Garde te Voet*, the first from the 'Gerpines' list of 1691 which confirms that blue coats were worn and secondly the somewhat less than reliable Wagner and Goldberg reference cards which show the facing to be red! The body of evidence does favour the orange facings, although the red cravat worn, by Angus McBride's reconstruction in the MAA on Marlborough's Army is less convincing (see Plate 1).

Flags

In the Royal Archives at Windsor Castle the following accounts details exist:

To the Rt. Honoble the Earle of Montagu & c
Colours for ye Dutch regiment of Footguardes
These and That you provide and deliver Six Colours for the Regiment of Dutch Guardes being made the Third Regiment of Guardes in the same manner and forme heretofore they used to be wch Regiment is Comanded by Count Solmes And this &c Dated the 10th day of July 1691 In the third year of their Mats Reigne.

October 21st 1691
Received then from their Mats Great Wardrobe as by Warrant Contra
Two Colours in the same manner and forme of Orange colour Taffata painted as heretoforewith two strings and Tassells and Two Ensigne Staves and Brasse nailes

A. Hyfvelf

December 8th 1691
Four Colours more with Strings Tassells Staves and gilt Nailes as aforesaid and Tenn yardes of Orange colour Galloone

N. Hoffmann

Thomas Waldron craves &c (including)
For ye Third Regiment of footguardes Commanded by Count Solmes For 6 Ensigne Staves with broad gilt heades at 8s Each
(dated 26th March 1692)

Thomas Holford craves &c
For the Third Regiment of Footguardes commanded by Count Solmes For making, gilding and painting Six Colours of Orange colour Taffat both sides alike painted with St Georges Crosse, Starr and Garter and other Trophies of Warr aft
12 each Colour   72
For 6 pair of Tassells of Silk with gold Cawles
and fringe att 7s each pair   22

26 March 1692 Montagu

Richard Bockenham craves &c
For ye Third Regiment of Footguardes Commanded by Count Solmes For 10
yardes of gold colour Silk Galoome for Six Colours aft 6d p yard

Colours for the Third Regimt of Foot Guards
Thesse &c that you provide and deliver six colours for the Regiment of Dutch
Guards being made the Third Regiment of Guards in the same manner and forme
as heretofore they used to be which Regiment is commanded by His Grace the
Duke of Wirtembergh. And this ande dated ye 27th of Aprile 1696 in the 8th Year
of his Maties Reigne

Aprile 27th 1696
Recieved from his Maties Grtt Wardrobe as by Warn Contra four Colours with
Staves and Tassells
M Lijt Velt

October 3d 1696
Recd more
Two Collours of Orange Collr mantua painted on both sides with Two Pair of
gold and orange Tassells, and Two Staves with guilded Spears

Richard Cooper and Partner craves &c
For Ensigne Colours for the 1st, 2d, 3d Regiments of Footguardes

for 104 Ells 3/4 of white florence Taffata: 18s	94 5 6
For 73 Ells 1/2 of Crimson florence Taffata 20s	73 10
For 37 yardes 1/2 of Orange Colours Mantua att 2s 22 10	

Gregorie King, Lancaster Herald craves allowance
For the Third Regimt of Footguardes Commanded by the Duke of Wirtemberg

For Making and Socketing 6 Ensignes aft l0s	3	
For 6 Ensigne Staves att l0s Each	3	
For 6 pair of Tassels Orange and Gold all 12s 6d		3 15
For Painting and Gilding all Over the Six		
Ensignes att 1.21 l0s 75		

Reconstructing the flags of the *Garde te Voet* from the above information
is no easy matter. No visual source exists for these colours and the possibly
contenders are deliberated during the comments below on Plate 2.

Part Two: Regiments of Foot

Organisation
With the exception of the *Garde te Voet*'s three battalions described in Part
One, the Nassau-Friesland Regiment (two battalions) and the two Stadtholder
Garde companies (Friesland and Groningen) all other Dutch regiments were

single battalion units. The battalion's organisation consisted of a staff and 12 companies formed as follows:

1 kapitein
1 luitenent
1 vendrig (ensign)
2 sergeants
2 tamboers (drummers)
1 Soliciteur (clerk)
3 Jongen (officers' servants)
60 corporals and private soldiers.

Likewise the staff consisted of a *kolonel*, one *luitenent-kolonel* (multiple battalion units such as Nassau-Friesland had an extra *luitenent-kolonel* to command the second battalion), one *majoor*, one *kwartiermeester* (quartermaster), one adjutant, one *predikant* (chaplain), one *veldsbeer* (surgeon) and one *soliciteur*. Companies were reduced to only 44 other ranks during peace time and then recruited up to full strength during 'mobilisation'. Unlike other armies of the time the Dutch grenadiers were not pulled together into one company, to serve on the flank, but were used as needs must as a small elite within each company.

However the regiment's pikemen, usually about one in five of the battalion's strength, at the beginning of the war were deployed together, as were the grenadiers in the *Garde te Voet* and the regiment Hornes-Kassel.

Dress and Equipment

To combat the generic vision that we have of the late-seventeenth/early-eighteenth century soldier and to put in its place a realistic individual image takes a leap of imagination that may, to mix metaphors, collapse like a house of cards. To create this image we have few hard facts and little illustration and those we do have appear at times to be contradictory. In the background of nearly every painting of William III, in heroic mode at the Boyne, there can be seen a small group of *Garde te Voet* moving away from us to cross the Boyne River. As I discussed in part one on the Dutch Foot Guards there is a consistency of dress and equipment, not only here, but in other paintings such as the various versions of the landing at Torbay which should show that the *Garde te Voet* wore cross belts in 1688. Whilst the evidence is pretty compelling, the danger is that most of these pictures are copies of a small body of work probably influenced by the engravings of Romeyn de Hooghe and therefore any errors are likely to have been repeated. Indeed these islandsare still infected with a mindless hero worship of William of Orange and the iconography continues still, with each new image created moving further both in quality and accuracy of reproduction and in originality of thought and behaviour from the original! Despite these reservations and although de Hooghe was primarily employed as a propagandist for William III there is enough truthful observation that can be tested in his work to believe thee image of the *Garde te Voet* in 1688 is an accurate one. Modern reconstructions by Frans Smit, painted in the late 1980s, are based on this premise, together with records of equipment issues. Smit does not, even at this early date show his musketeers equipped with collars of charges, they have a large, rather shapeless, cartouche hanging low on their right hip, mirrored by a sword at the same height on the shoulder belt on the opposite side. Indeed shapeless is a word that could be used to describe much of what Smits sees in Dutch soldiers of this period.

The two other good sources also reflect the air of scruffiness which may have been the Dutch soldier's lot. A de Hooghe engraving entitled 'William III arriving at Het Loo with his Guards' shows the King, surrounded by horsemen, entering the gates of his palace, while a regiment of infantry is drawn up to salute him. The implication is that these are the *Garde te Voet*, in which case they now have waist belts for their swords, but still wear shapeless hats and look as if their clothes are a few sizes too large. However, this is also very obviously the source for Knotel's plate on the regiment Friesheim and therefore more questions are in need of answers: did Knotel know something about the plate which points to the regiment being Friesheim, or did a similarity of the flag draw him to that conclusion? The accuracy of Knotel's plate is particularly important as it has influenced everyone describing the Dutch soldier of this period and has been repeated by everyone from Preben Kannik to Angus McBride in the Michael Barthorp Osprey Men at Arms book on Marlborough! The final visual source to be considered is the pen and watercolour study in the Royal collection. This depicts four soldiers facing forward muskets over their shoulders with a variety of headgear. I have attempted to illustrate the headgear in Plate 3, so I will limit my comments here to general remarks about the cut of their coats and their equipment. The original attribution, based on a note on the back, was to the Dutch artist Allaert van Everdingen (1621–75). This has been revised as he died long before any reasonable date for the dress of the soldiers. J.G. Kerkhoven of the Koninklijk Nederlands Leger-en Wapenmusuem in Delft suggests a date of 1702, which seems more likely. If it is, then these still somewhat untidy representatives of William III's infantry are now equipped with waist belts for sword and plug bayonet, plus a shoulder belt for their still rather shapeless cartouche. However, the inclusion of the plug bayonet probably dates them slightly earlier. A likely narrative could proceed as follows: the Dutch soldiers who came to England in 1688 wore crossed shoulder belts, these had replaced collars of charges sometime after 1680. Between 1688 and the height of the Nine Years' War a waist belt replaced one of the shoulder belt, thus allowing the plug bayonet to be carried. I think this points to the picture in the Royal collection being earlier than Kerkhoven's attribution, probably around 1692–5 as plug bayonets were rather outmoded by 1702. That these few sources are the best we have shows the paucity of information available and even in the best of these, the picture in the Royal collection, locks on the musket are rather confusing, appearing to be flintlocks pointing backwards in the manner of matchlock serpentines whilst being attached to the wrong side of the musket stocks. So if our source couldn't draw a musket, why should we trust the rest of his observations? Finally, concerning the dress of a regiment pikemen it would appear they were dressed as musketeers minus the latter's equipment, they may have worn armour, as de Hooghe's illustrations of militia show back- and breast-plates being worn, but this is unfortunately not conclusive.

Below are listed the known infantry regiments of the Dutch army of the period. To enable cross-referencing they are numbered using the system in Alan Sapherson's book. However, Dutch infantry were not yet numbered but were known simply by the name of their colonel. Responsibility for the funding of these regiments was shared out amongst the provinces of the Netherlands, with the larger and more affluent such as Holland taking the lion's share. These provinces seem to have been proud of their regiments and many displayed the provincial arms on their colours. During the period in question a Dutch infantry battalion would be expected to carry three colours, usually the colonel's, lieutenant-colonel's and major's. During the war this was at some point, reduced to two. The colonel's colour would normally have a white background, with all other colours having usually the same design but with a colour other than white as a background.

The Regiments of Foot

(1) Formed 1602
Colonels:
    1688 Willem van BULOW
    1695 Stephen van WELDEREN (Brigadier 1702)
Maintained by Gelderland
Dress: see Plate 4

(2) Formed 1674
Colonels:
    1678 Ditmar van WIJNBERGEN (Major-General 1691; Governor of
    Bergen-op-Zoom 1694)
    1696 Johann van BEIJNHELM (Brigadier 1702)
Maintained by Gelderland
Dress: see Plate 4

(3) Formed 1622
Colonels:
    1682 Filips van ESSEN Heer van den Burgh
    1698 Maurits Henrik van PLATTENBERG (Brigadier 1702)
Maintained by Gelderland
Dress: see Plate 4

(4) *Garde te Voet* (Foot Guards) see Part One

(5) Formed 1586
Colonels:
    1672 Georg Frederik furst von WALDECK-PYRMONT (1st Field Marshal
    1688 Commanding General Anglo-Dutch forces, 1688–90)
    1693 Johann Adolf Herzog von HOLSTEIN-PLON (was 1st Field Marshal
    in 1693, Governor of Maastricht. 1693: captured Huy 1694)

Maintained by Holland
Dress: see Plate 4

(6) Formed 1602
Colonels:
    1678 Graf Willem Adriaan van HORNES Baron van KESSEL (Master
    General of Dutch Artillery 1672–1694
    1694 Philippe Claude Touroud de ST. AMANT (Brigadier 1702)
Maintained by Holland
Dress: see Plate 4

(7) Formed 1671
Colonels:
    1678 Henrik van DELWICH vrijherr van Wiebendoff (Lieutenant-General
    1688)
    1692 Karel LINDEBOOM (Major-General 1695)
Maintained by Holland
Dress: see Plate 4

(8) Formed 1672
Colonels:
    1673 Johann Karl, Prins Palzgraf von BIRKENFELD (Lieutenant General
    1688)
Maintained by Holland
Dress: see Plate 3

(9) Formed 1668
Colonels:
    1688 Karel MANMAEKER Heer van Hofwegen
    1689 Willem van HEUCKELEM Heer van Crommestyn (Major-General
    1695)
Maintained by Holland
Dress: no information available

(10) Formed 1643
Colonels:
    1688 Johann van BEAUMONT
    1695 Menno Baron COEHOORN (Major-General 1692; Lieutenant
    General 1695)
Maintained by Holland
Dress: see Plate 4

(11) Formed 1599
Colonels:
    1678 Daniel de Tassin de TORSAY (Major-General 1688)
Maintained by Holland
Dress: see Plate 4

(12) Formed 1666
Colonels:
   1682 Meynard de PERCEVAL
   1691 Coert Jan van SWANSBEL (Brigadier 1701)
Maintained by Holland
Dress: see Plate 4 (this regiment became Marines in 1698)

(13) Formed 1671
Colonels:
   1673 Nicholaas Frederik ZOBEL (Major-General 1691)
   1695 Johann Wynand van GOOR (Major-General 1701: commanded
   Dutch artillery train in England 1688 and Flanders after 1690)
Maintained by Holland
Dress: see Plate 4

(14) Formed 1673
Colonels:
   1688 Ernst Willem van SALISCH (Major-General 1694; Lieutenant-
   General 1697; General 1705)
Maintained by Holland
Dress: see Plate 4

(15) Formed 1673
Colonels:
   1674 Nicholaas Francis FAGEL (Major-General 1694; Lieutenant-General
   1701)
Maintained by Holland
Dress: see Plate 4

(16) Formed 1665
Colonels:
   1674 Johann Belgicus, Graaf van HORNES-BOXTEL
   1695 Willem van SOUTELANDE (Brigadier 1702)
Dress: see Plate 4

(17) Date unknown
Colonels:
   1675 Frederik Johann van Baer, Heer van SLANGENBURG (Major-
   General 1683; Lieutenant-General 1692)
Dress: see Plate 4

(18) Formed 1673
Colonels:
   1673 Prinz Albrecht Friedrich Von BRANDENBURG (brother of the
   Elector Friedrich, later king in Prussia. Prinz Albrecht was only a year old
   at the time of his appointment)
Maintained by Holland, but paid for by England 1688–97
Dress: see Plate 5

(19) Formed 1668
Colonels:
    1676 William Florentin, Rijngmaf van SALM
    1695 Johann Frederik Graaf van DOHNA-FERASSIERES (Brigadier 1701)
Maintained by Holland
Dress: see Plate 4

(20) Formed 1600
Colonels:
    1688 Ferdinand van der Gracht Heer van L'ECLUSE (Major General 1694)
    1695 Print Walrad von NASSAU-SAARBRUCKEN-USINGEN (2nd Field
    Marshal 1688)
    1701 Prinz Wilhelm Heinrich von NASSAU-SAARBRUCKEN-USINGEN
Maintained by Holland
Dress: see Plate 5

(21) Date Unknown
Colonels:
    1679 Samuel de LANNOY
    1692 Amault van der MEULEN, Heer van Schoonenburg
    1694 Print Joachim Friedrich von HOLSTEIN-NORBURG
Maintained by Holland
Dress: see Plate 5

(22) Formed 1665
Colonels:
    Henrik van Uytenhoven, Heer van AMELISWEERD
Maintained by Holland
Dress: see Plate 5

Formed 1644
Colonels:
    1680 Wahad, Graaf van NASSAU-SAARBRUCKEN-OTTWEILER
    (Major-General 1691; Lieutenant-General 1699; Colonel of the *Garde te
    Voet* 1701)
    1701 Rainier Vincent VAN DER BEKE (Brigadier 1702)
Maintained by Zealand, but paid for by England 1688–97
Dress: see Plate 5

(24) Formed 1664
Colonels:
    1680 Jacques Louis, Comte de NOYELLES-FALAIS (Major-General 1691;
    Lieutenant-General 1694)
Maintained by Zealand
Dress: see Plate 5

(25) Formed 1664
Colonels:

1664 Simon SCHOTIE
1692 Johann CAU 1697 Carl Wilhelm Baron von SPARRE (Major-General 1702)
Maintained by Zealand
Dress: no information available (regiment became marines 1698)

(26) Formed 1672
Colonels:
    1688 Assuerus SCHIMMELPENNICK van der Oye, Heer van Kell
    1693 Christiaan ARENTS
    1701 Johann de VASSY
Maintained by Zealand
Dress: see Plate 5

(27) Formed 1672
Colonels:
    1674 Henrik van WEEDE (Major-General 1688)
    1700 Comelis van NASSAU, Heer van WOUDENBURG
Maintained by Utrecht
Dress: see Plate 5

(28) Formed 1665
Colonels:
    1680 Francois de RAM Heer van HAGEDOORN
    1691 Daniel Maximillian de Herteing, Heer van MARQUETTE
    1699 Johann Wemer, Baron van PALLANDT
Maintained by Utrecht
Dress: see Plate 5

(29) Formed 1672
Colonels:
    1675 Prinz Friedrich August von BRALINSCHWEIG-LÜNEBURG-OSNABRUCK
    1691 Hendrik Vrijheer van FRIESEN
    1692 Julius Ernst von TETTAU (Lieutenant-General 1692)
    1697 Johann Rabo van KEPPEL
Maintained by Utrecht till 1697 and then by Holland
Dress: see Plate 5

(30) Date Unknown
Colonels:
    1684 Rutger van HAERSOLTE
    1701 Wilhelm Konstantinos, Wildgraaf und Rheingraaf von SALM
    1701 Coenraad RANCK
Maintained by Utrecht
Dress: see Plate 5

(31) Formed 1672
Colonels:
    1672 Paul du BAYE, Heer van THEIL (Major-General 1691)
    1699 Frans Jacob, Baron van WAES, Heer van Kesseulch
Dress: see Plate 5

(32) Date unknown
COMPAGNIE GARDE van den STADHOUDER FRIESLAND. A single
company of 200 men usually brigaded with the *Garde te Voet*
Captain commanding:
    1667 Johann Coenders
Maintained by Friesland
Dress: probably blue coat lined in red (see also 41, below)

(33) Formed 1660s
Colonels:
    Prinz Henrik Casimir, Stadhouder van NASSAUFRIESLAND (Prinz van
    Nassau-Dietz 1657–96; cousin to William III; Field Marshal 1688)
    1696 Prinz Johann Willem Frisco, Stadhoeder van NASSAU-FRIESLAND
    (Prinz van Nassau Dietz 1686–1711, son of the above, Prince of Orange
    1708–11)
Maintained by Friesland
Dress: see Plate 5 (this unit was also called 'Friesland-Garde')

(34) Formed 1577
Colonels:
    1659 Haas Willem van AYLVA (Major-General 1668; Lieutenant-General
    1672; Lieutenant-Admiral of Friesland)
    1691 Hesse van AYLVA
    1694 Williem Frederik, Baron van SCHRATENBACH (Brigadier 1701)
Maintained by Friesland
Dress: see Plate 5

(35) Formed 1633
Colonels:
    1674 Watzo van BURMANIA
    1691 Johann Wilhelm II, Herzog von SAXE-EISENACH (1666–1729,
    married William III's cousin Amelia in 1691)
Maintained by Friesland
Dress: no details available

(36) Formed 1671
Colonels:
    1686 Cornelis van SCHELTINGA
    1699 Frederik VEGELIN van Claerbergen
Maintained by Friesland
Dress: see Plate 5

(37) Formed 1644
Colonels:
   1683 Albert, Graaf van LIMBURG-STYRUM-BRONCKHORST
   1690 Menno Baron COEHORN (see 10 above)
   1695 Gozewyn van COEHORN
   1695 Gideon van COEHORN
Maintained by Friesland
Dress: see Plate 5

(38) Formed 1672
Colonels:
   1686 Julius van BEYMA
   1698 Joachim van AMAMA (Brigadier 1702)
Maintained by Friesland
Dress: in 1693 the regiment ordered 603 ells of red kersey (probably for lining)

(39) Formed 1632
Colonels:
   1678 Otto Philip van COEVERDE
   1690 Johann Diederik, Baron van HEYDE
Maintained by Overijssel
Dress: see Plate 5

(40) Formed 1672
Colonels:
   1683 Guslav CARLSON, Graaf von Bornig Heer von Lindtholm
   1689 Hans Wolf van GRABEN
   1690 Lodewijk Frederik van AUER
   1695 Ernst Ledewijk WILCKE (Brigadier 1702)
Maintained by Overijssel, but paid for by England 1688–97
Dress: copper buttons, no other details

(41) Formed 1595
COMPAGNIE van der STADHOUDER GRONINGEN (see 32 above for details)
Captain commanding:
   1658 Rempt Ten Ham van Holtzappel
   1690 Nicholaas Blance
Maintained by Groningen
Dress: see 32 above for details

(42) Formed 1654
Colonels:
   1681 Henrik LOSECAET
Maintained by Groningen
Dress no details available

(43) Formed 1595
STADHOUDER GRONINGEN / REGIMENT STAD EN LAND GRONINGEN
(the regiment of the Stadtholder of Groningen, an office held until his death by
William III's cousin)
Colonels:
  1675 Prinz Henrik Casimir. Stadhouder van GRONINGEN (see 33 above)
  1696 Rempt TEN HAM van Holtzappel (see 41 above). It appears that after
  1696 the regiment was known only as Ten Ham after its colonel
Maintained by Groningen
Dress: see Plate 5

(44) Formed 1671
Colonels:
  Barent van PROTT
Maintained by Groningen
Dress: see Plate 5

(45) Formed 1672
Colonels:
  Vacant until 1696, known by the name of the previous colonel, Ter
  Bruggen. Georg Gebbard Linstau served as lieutenant-colonel
  commanding
  1696 Georg Gebbard van LINSTAU, previously lieutenant-colonel
Maintained by Drenthe (Groningen)
Dress: see Plate 5

(46) Formed 1689
Colonels:
  1689 Conrad Willem DEDEM (Major-General 1701)
Maintained by Holland until 1698 and then by Utrecht
Dress: no information available

(47) Formed 1689
Colonels:
  1689 Joachim Wille van CLAUBERGEN
  1693 Tobias REYNARD
Maintained firstly by Zealand, then Gelderland and Friesland and finally
(after 1702) by Groningen
Dress: no details available

(48) Formed 1689
Colonels:
  1689 Hugo de BRAUW, Heer van Ketel
Maintained by Holland and then by Groningen
Dress: no details available

(49) Formed 1690
Colonels:

1690 Gerriit baron HEECKEREN
1695 Egmond van ELS (Brigadier 1702)
Maintained jointly by Utrecht and Gelderlaed until 1701 and then by Utrecht and Holland
Dress: see Plate 5

(50) Formed 1690
Colonels:
1690 Johann Theodore, Baron van FRIESHEIM (Major-General 1701)
Maintained by Holland
Dress: see Plates 4 and 5

(51) Formed 1690
Colonels:
1690 Otto GOES (killed in action 1692)
1692 Anthony Gunter Prinz von HOLSTEIN-BECK
Maintained by Holland until 1698 and then by Zealand
Dress: see Plate 5

Part Three: Guard and Line Cavalry

During the period in question (1688–1702) the Dutch cavalry were almost as well respected as their infantry. Like their infantry the Dutch cavalry often got the better of their more numerous French opponents with a combination of superior discipline and tactical doctrine. The French were indeed undergoing a period of tactical debate with an ongoing war fought out between the supporters of cavalry firepower and the use of some form of 'caracole' tactic and those who endorsed the benefits of 'cold steel'. The latter tactic, whilst seeming to our modern eyes in retrospect the most effective, often left all but the most well-disciplined forces in disarray!

The Dutch managed to retain the best features of both system, by keeping the body of horse together by advancing at an regular pace (probably the ubiquitous 'good round Trott' until at pistol range they would discharge their weapons and charge home! At what pace this 'charge' was delivered is difficult to judge, however given effective pistol ranges were extremely short it is hard to see them reaching even a canter before contact was made. It is fair to say that the effectiveness of the Dutch tactics lay not in the speed of delivery but in the cohesion which not only allowed a unit to win an initial victory over its opponent but also triumph in the successive engagements as more lines of troops became involved. The aspect of discipline was critical to the final result and here in particular the Dutch were superior. Both these superiorities, radical and disciplinary, was passed on to the British allies so that by the time of Marlborough's campaigns both armies were able to field very effective forces of cavalry. Sadly, while the British cavalry, with a few exceptions, retained its reputation throughout the eighteenth century the Dutch declined to such a degree that by the War of the Austrian Succession the Dutch cavalry was a spent force which failed badly at Fontenoy in 1744.

Regiments and their Organisation

In 1688 the Dutch horse consisted of 25 formations, this included the two Guard cavalry regiments (one of which contained two independent companies) and 22 line cavalry regiments. The latter were usually formed from a regimental staff and six companies. These were deployed on the battlefield in two squadrons. Usual campaigning strength for a two-squadron Dutch cavalry regiment was around 350 officers and men, although in theory the numbers should have been closer to 410.

Each company consisted of the following:
  1 rittmeester (captain)
  1 luitenent
  1 kornet (cornet)
  1 kwartiermeester (quartermaster)
  1 tromptter (trumpeter)
  1 hoefsmid (blacksmith)
  1 schrijver (company clerk)
  60 ratters (troopers)

Each of the troopers, together with the trumpeter, blacksmith and clerk, had one horse, whilst the officers had the following entitlement: captain six, lieutenant four, cornet three, quartermaster two.

The two Guard regiments differed from the line, the *Garde te Paard* in some minor details and the *Garde du Corps* considerably. The *Garde te Paard* (Horse Guards) consisted of nine companies rather than six which was the norm in the line. There were also two more troopers in each company and an additional trumpeter, but no blacksmith. This gave the *Garde te Paard* a minimal strength of 630 officers and men. However unlike the line cavalry regiment this size seems to have been maintained on campaign giving the *Garde te Paard* the numbers nearly equal to two line regiments.

The *Garde du Corps* was formed from two separate companies; the *Garde du Corps* of 'Zijne Majesteit' the Prince of Orange and that of the Stadhouder of Friesland and Groningen. The 'Zijne Majesteit' company consisted of 197 officers and men and the Friesland/Groningen company 175. The members of these companies were considered to be elite and their rank and privileges within the army were higher than their rank within their companies. Therefore the Captain-Commandant of the *Garde du Corps* of Friesland and Groningen ranked as a colonel, the lieutenant as a lieutenant-colonel and the cornet and guidon bearers as majors.

Following the outbreak of war several new regiments were raised. Firstly in 1689 following the example of the French army men from each company, of every regiment were withdrawn to form a new Karabiniers regiment. The new regiment had six slightly smaller companies of 50 men each deployed in two squadrons. In 1701, prior to the War of the Spanish Succession, this was increased to 10 companies, one of which was dressed as horse grenadiers. Also three regiments in the service of the Duke of Württemberg were taken into Dutch pay and in 1693 three more units of native Dutch horse were formed. Finally in 1701, as well as enlarging the Karabiniers, King William raised three more regiments of cavalry, to counter the threat from France.

Dress and Equipment

Though uniforms of the Dutch cavalry followed much the same style as that worn by troops all over Europe. The large coat or *justacorps* was normally grey and collarless with a coloured lining and large cuffs which also showed the lining material. Hats were often, but not always black and could have anything from one in three sides turned up. The paintings of Dutch artists such as Jan de Wyck and Jan van Huchtenburgh are useful in helping to get a feel for the period and the dress of the participants. Sometimes it is difficult to 'pin down' the specific regiments depicted but often clues can be spotted that can be very useful, like his infantry counterpart the Dutch cavalryman seems to have adopted an air of studied scruffiness and as noted above, hats do not always seem to have been of one consistent colour within a regiment. This would have been unthinkable in the French army in which the King demanded a greater level of uniformity (note: Louis XIV seems to have had a pathological hatred of grey hats in particular. For a specific example of this see the part of St. Simon's memories relating to the Army review of 1699!)

Additionally there are a number of examples of weird and wonderful types of head dress amongst William's officers and these will be discussed in the plates section. Armour seems to have been worn by some officers but not by the men. although most troopers probably wore a protective 'secret' in their hats. Black 'jacked' boots were worm with white metal spurs. For equipment the Dutch troops of 1688–90 probably wore 'crossed belts' as these are universally depicted during this period, one over the left shoulder suspended the firearm and the one over the right the sword. There is no pictorial evidence that the cavalry followed the practice in the infantry and went over to waist belts, and there is such a paucity of sources that this cannot be taken for granted. Sashes, or scarfs as they were known during the period, seem to have been in the house colour of orange and worn around the waist.

The Regiments

I have used the numbering sequence used by C.A. Sapherson in his excellent book on William III's Dutch Army. In reality the regiments were known by their proprietor's name. Those in English service are rendered in bold italics.

(1) Formed 1671
Maintained by Gelderland
Colonels:
    03/10/83 Frederick Willem. Baron de HEYDEN. Killed in Action 1690
    23/09/90 Henrik van ITTERSUM
    4/09/96 Frederik Christiaan van Reede. Baron AUGHRIM
Uniform: see Plate 8

(2) Formed 1672
Maintained by Holland, in English Service 1688–98
GARDES TE PAARD

Colonels:

05/06/74 Hans Willem Bentinck. Earl of PORTLAND

07/08/01 Henri du Massue. Marquis de Ruvigny, Earl of GALWAY

The regiment is often referred to as 'Lord Portland's Horse'

Uniform: See Plate 6

(3) Formed 1671

Maintained by Holland

Colonels:

03/04/79 Prins Walrad van NASSAU-SAARBRUCKEN-USINGEN

21/10/01 Johan Karel van ECK

Uniform: see Plates 7 and 8

(4) Formed 1671

Maintained by Holland

Colonels:

1671 Claude T'Serclaes, Graaf van TILLY

Uniform: white coat lined red (from Gerpines)

(5) Formed 1672

Maintained by Holland, in English Service 1688–97

Colonels:

08/02/72 Armand de Caumont de la Force, Marquis de
MONTPOUILLAN

21/11/97 Armand de Caumount Marquis de MADURAN

Uniform: white coat lined white (from Belaubre)

(6) Formed 1645

Maintained by Holland

Colonels:

Jacob van Wassenaar Heed van OBDAM

Uniform: grey coat lined scarlet or red (Tilroy and Gerpines)

(7) Formed 1672

Maintained by Holland, in English Service 1688–97

Colonels:

01/07/79 Willem Frederik van NASSAU-ZUYLENSTEIN

Uniform: probably white coats

(8) Formed 1672

Maintained by Holland

Colonels:

08/02/72 Adriaan Gustaaf, Graaf van FLODOR 15/99 Johann de RHOO

Uniform: grey coat lined scarlet or red (Tilroy and Gerpines)

(9) Formed 1635

Maintained by Holland

Colonels:

23/02/67 George Frederik, Graaf yon WALDECK-PYRMONT
14/01/93 Ernest Frederik Herzog von SAXE-HEILBURG-
HILDBURGHHAUSEN
Uniform: see Plate 8

(10) Formed 1672
Maintained by Holland, in English Service 1688–97
Colonels:
03/08/76 Albert Ferdinand. Graaf van BERLO
14/10/90 Johann Rejnhard HOORNBERGH
Uniform: see Plate 8

(11) Formed 1635
Maintained by Holland
Colonels:
14/01/84 Floris Karel van Beyeren Schagen, Graaf van WARFUSE
26/5/99 Lubbert van ECK
Uniform: see Plate 8

(12) Formed 1672
Maintained by Holland, in English Service 1688–97
Colonels:
15/10/75 Willem Roelman. Vrijeer Quadt SOPPENBROEK
25/12/88 Paul Didier de BONCOURT
16/08/01 Johann de Fagel van Assendelft, Heer van CRALINGEN
Uniform: no details

(13) Formed 1672
Maintained by Holland
Colonels:
03/01/84 Henrik BENTINCK Heer van Diepanheim
27/02/91 Nicholaas de DOMPRE
Uniform: white coat lined blue (Tilroy)

(14) Formed 1672
Maintained by Holland, in English service 1689–97
Colonels:
06/10/88 George Baron de RIEDESEL
1688 Gerard PIJPER
23/04/98 Frederik Ulrich, Graaf van OOST-FRIESLAND
Uniform: no details

(15) Formed 1594
Maintained by Holland, in English service 1688–97
Colonels:
23/03/69 Adam van der Duyn, Heer van S'GRAVEMOER
01/01/94 Zeno Diederick TENGNAGEL, Heer van Gelicum
Uniform: grey lined green (Belaubre)

(16) Formed 1672
Maintained by Holland, in English Service 1688–97
Colonels:
    24/12/81 Bogislaff Sigismund SCHACK
Uniform: no details

(17) Formed 1688
Maintained by Holland
Colonels:
    9/10/88 Nicholaas van der Duyn, Heer van RYSWUK
    25/3/98 Maurits Lodwijk van NASSAU-BEVERWEED-LA LECK
Uniform: white coat lined white (Tilroy and Gerpines)

(18) Formed 1635
Maintained by Holland, in English Service 1688–97
Colonels:
    03/10/73 Matthias Hoefft van OYEN
    14/05/91 Johann Zeger van RECHTEREN
Uniform: see Plate 8

(19) Formed 1599
Maintained by Zealand, in English Service 1688–99
GARDE DU CORP VAN ZIJNE MAJESVIEIT
Captain Commandant: Henrik van Nassau-Ouwerkirk
Uniforms: see Plate 6

(20) Formed 1672
Maintained by Zealand
Colonels:
    24/10/72 Johann Theobald Metzger van WEYNBOM
    26/02/91 Johann de HUYBERT, Heer van Noordgouwe
    12/04/01 Henrick Frederik Paul de RAMMINGEN
Uniform: see Plate 8

(21) Formed 1635
Maintained by Utrecht, in English Service 1688–97
Colonels:
    04/5/35 Godard van GINKEL Earl of ATHLONE (from 1690)
Uniforms: see Plate 8

(22) Formed 1668
Maintained by Friesland
GARDE DU CORPS VAN DEN STADHOUDER NASSAU-FRIESLAND
Captain-Commandant: Hilken van Lorch
Uniform: see Plate 6

(23) Formed 1668
Maintained by Friesland (known as Friesland-Garde)

Colonels:
  20/12/73 Prins Hennk Casimir van NASSAU-FRIESLAND
  28/03/96 Prins Johann Willem Friso van ORANJE-NASSAU
Uniform: see Plate 8

(24) Formed 1672
Maintained by Overijssel, in English Service 1688–97
Colonels:
  1683 Otto, Graaf van der LIPPE
  18/02/90 Robert van Ittersum. Heer van NIEUWENHUIS
  14/9/92 Otto Frededk VITTINGHOFF Heer van Needermeert
Uniform: no details

(25) Formed 1635 Maintained by Groningen
Colonels:
  27/02/77 Frederik Willem VAN BER BORGH killed in action 1690
  21/04/92 Prins Frederick Jacob yon HESSE-HOMBERG
Uniform: grey-white coat lined red (Gerpines and Belaubre)

(26) 1ST WÜRTTEMBURG REGIMENT. Taken into Dutch Service 1688
Maintained by Holland until 1690 and then Gelderland
Colonels:
  19/11/88 Harman Frederik von ERFFA
  01/01/90 Duke Ernst of SAXE-HEILBURG-HILDURGHAUSEN
  12/07/92 Philip Ludwig von ERBACH
Uniform: white coat lined in green (Tilroy and Gerpines)

(27) 2nd WÜRTTEMBURG REGIMENT. Taken into Dutch Service 1688
Maintained by Zealand
Colonels:
  02/12/88 Veit Heinrich TRUCHESS von Westhausen
  25/02/89 Philip Landgrave von HESSE-DARMSTADT
  20/10/94 Hans Adolf, Duke of HOLSTEIN-PLON
Uniform: see Plate 8

(28) 3rd WÜRTTEMBURG REGIMENT. Taken into Dutch Service 1688
Maintained by Zealand
Colonels:
  02/12/88 Prince Friedrich Heinrich von WÜRTTEMBURG
  03/03/93 Prince Friedrich Karl von WÜRTTEMBURG
  20/10/94 Prince Friedrich Heinrich von WÜRTTEMBURG
Uniform: see Plate 8

(29) Formed 1689 (see text for details). Maintained by Holland
REGIMENT KARABINIERS
Colonels:
  11/01/89 Frederic Adolf, Graf van LIPPE
  25/05/95 Arnold Joost van Kepple, Earl of ALBERMARLE

Uniform: see Plate 8

(30) Formed 1693 (Raised in Spanish Netherlands)
Maintained by Holland
Colonels:
    29/05/93 Nicholas Francois, Baron de CHAVIRAY
    28/11/97 Alexandre de BAY
    19/04/01 Denis Francois Urbain de Retz de Bruscila de CHANCLOS
Uniform: no details

(31) Formed 1693 (Raised in Spanish Netherlands)
Maintained by Holland
Colonels:
    06/06/93 Philippe Joseph, Baron de GRISPERRE
    20/06/98 Jean, Comte de NYSLE
Uniform: no details

(32) Formed 1693 (Raised in Spanish Netherlands)
Maintained by Holland
Colonels:
    01/06/93 Francois Louis de MONFLIN
Uniform: no details

(33) Formed 1701
Maintained by Friesland
Colonels:
    04/04/01 Frederik Sirtema van GROVESTINS
Uniform: no details

(34) Formed 1701
Maintained by Friesland
Colonels:
    1701 Frans Mende van ENIGMA
Uniform: no details

(35) Formed 1701
Maintained by Friesland
Colonels:
    1701 Hans Jurrien de BALDWIN
Uniform: no details

Part Four: Dragoons and Artillery

Dragoons
By the end of Malborough's wars probably only the French, of the major European nations, still used their dragoons in the traditional role with those of most other armies as purely cavalry.

The Regiments

In 1968, when the war broke out, the Dutch dragoon force consisted of the Guard Dragoons and Marwitz's, however Berlo's was raised the same year and in 1693 a further regiment, Mattha's was formed. After the treaty of Ryswick in 1697 brought the wars to a close the dragoon companies were reduced to a strength of 40 men and two whole regiments were dismounted. In 1701, when tension began to grow over the Spanish succession crisis the companies were built up to full strength and the horses returned.

(1) Formed 1672
Maintained by England 1688–1698
THE REGIMENT GARDE DRAGONDERS
Colonels:

   1678 William III, King of Great Britain and Ireland, Prince of Orange and Stadtholder of the United Provinces. 16/09/02 Wilhelm, Prinz von Hesse-Kessel

Note: This regiment was normally known by the name of its commander in the field, its colonel-commandant Abraham van Eppinger, and is referred to hereafter as EPPINGER'S Dragoons.
Uniform: see Plate 9

(2) Formed 1672
Maintained by all the provinces
Colonels:

   02/02/88 Christoffel van MARWITZ
   23/06/93 Christoffel van SCHLIPPENBACK
Uniform: see Plate 9

(3) Formed 1688
Maintained by all the provinces
Colonels:

   25/10/88 Albert Ferdinand, Graf van BERLO
   23/11/89 George Frederik, Graf van WALDECK-PYRMONT

Organisation

The Dutch dragoon force was not as numerically strong as the cavalry and infantry of William III's army, consisting of only four regiments. One of these was the regiment Garde Dragoons of which William III was the colonel, this was a particularly strong regiment with 10 companies making up five squadrons in total.

   A company of dragoons was organised as follows. Each company consisted of the following:

   1 kapitain (captain)
   1 luitenent
   1 vendrig (cornet)
   2 sergeants
   1 tamboer (drummer)

1 schrijver (company clerk)
3 jongens (officers' servants)
69 dragonders (dragoons)

Whilst the Guard had 10 companies in five squadrons, the others had eight companies in four squadrons. This gave them an official strength of 648 men, the Guard Dragoons 800.

During this period the dragoon was changing from a mounted infantrymen into a fully fledged cavalryman. Earlier the dragoons had been equipped with poor quality 'nags' which they rode onto the battlefield, were deployed and dismounted to fight. However by the 1690s whilst the dismounted role had not entirely been abandoned they were being more regularly used as cavalrymen, albeit ones that were not as highly regarded as the real thing.

Artillery
Until 1689 Dutch artillery consisted of four companies each containing 102 artillery handlers. In that year a fifth company was formed and in 1690 the company strength was increased to 260 men. For this period the full details of the complement is incomplete, however there were 142 handlers and carpenters.

More detail is available for 1701 when a reduced company of 138 was made up of:

1 kapitain
1 luitenent
3 under-luitenents
4 master fireworkers
4 bombardiers
46 constables (gun captains)
1 corporal carpenter
10 carpenters
4 corporal gun handlers
62 gun handlers
2 officers' servants

The artillery personnel, for obvious safety reasons, were armed with flintlocks rather than matchlocks.

The Pontoon Company
A total of 77 men, the company was attached to the artillery:

1 kapitain
2 luitenents
6 corporals
2 tinsmiths

Part Five: William's Allies and Generals

To complete this survey of the Dutch army of William of Orange this article consists of a series of 'pen' portraits of William's allies and generals. Throughout the period of his wars against the might of Louis XIV, William attempted to form as wide a coalition as possible of those opposed to the aims of the 'Sun King'. In 1672 this series of wars had begun when Louis attempted to invade the Netherlands with the complicity of Great Britain and with the Dutch alone. However by the end of tbe war, six years later, not only had Britain changed sides but a number of others such as Brandenburg and Hesse had sprung up to aid the Dutch. Many of these countries remained allied to the Dutch and some of their rulers became important leaders in the armies of the coalition.

AHLEFELDT, Frederik (1662–1708), Danish
He served as a colonel in the Danish contingent sent to Ireland in 1690. Promoted to brigadier in 1692, and major-general in 1695.

ALBEMARLE, Arnold Joost van Keppel (1669–1718), Dutch
Favourite, and probably lover of the King. Major-General from 1697.

During the War of the Spanish Succession commanded the Dutch at the defeat at Denain. William had earlier made him inspector of his Swiss troops.

AYLVA, Hans Willem, Baron van (d.1691), Dutch
Very experienced soldier who was a major-general as early as 1668 and a lieutenant-general in 1672.

BAVARIA, Maximilian-Emmanuel von Wittelsbach, Elector of (1662–1736), German
Succeeded as Elector in 1679. Fought against the Turks during the campaigns of the 1680s. Served as governor of the Spanish Netherlands in the 1690s, as a result of his continued support for the Habsburgs. Dramatically changed sides in time to fight for the French during the War of the Spanish Succession. He was then expelled from his Electorate following the French defeat at Blenheim in 1704. Ironically he then served as the French appointee in the Spanish Netherlands. whilst exiled from his own country. His possessions were restored by the Treaty of Utrecht in 1714.

BERLO, Albert Ferdinand van (d.1690), Dutch
Appointed colonel in 1676 and brigadier in 1688.

COEHOORN, Menno, Baron van (1634–1704), Dutch
Served at the siege of Maastricht in 1673. Conducted the siege of Bonn, under the Elector of Brandenburg in 1689. Promoted brigadier in 1690 and lieutenant-general in 1695, for his success in recapturing Namur. Created Engineer-General of Fortifications in the same year and Master-General of Dutch artillery in 1697. Along with Vauban undoubtedly the major figure in engineering and siege warfare during the seventeenth century.

DOPFF, Daniel Wolf van (1655–1718), Dutch
Favourite of Waldeck (q.v.) was deputy quartermaster-general in 1676 and later, in 1687, quartermaster-general of the cavalry. Colonel of dragoons at the beginning of the Nine Years' War, he was promoted quartermaster-general and major-general, as well as governor of Maastricht in 1694. He was a lieutenant-general in 1701.

ELLENBURG, Johann Anton (1637–1695), German
Born in Hesse. Served in the Danish army and was promoted brigadier in 1690. He was a major-general by the following year but following his failure to provide a more spirited defence of Dixmuyde, in 1695 he, like Byng 50 years later, was executed 'pour encourager l'autres'.

FAGEL, Francis Nicholaas, Baron (1632 pour encourager l'autres' 1706). Dutch
A major-general in 1694, Fagel was promoted to lieutenant-general in 1701.

FLODROFF, Adriaan. Count van (d.1690), Dutch
Entered the army in 1671 and by 1683 was a major-general of cavalry. He was killed at the Battle of Reurus in 1690.

FEIESLAND, Henrik Casimir II van Nassau-Dietz, Prince of (d.1696), Dutch
A cousin of the King, who was also Stadtholder of Friesland and Groningen, he was third field marshal in the Dutch Army in 1689, resigning in 1692.

GINKEL, Godart van, 1st Earl of Athlone (1630–1703), Dutch
Born and died in Utrecht. Ginkel was a major-general in 1675, a lieutenant-general in 1683 and a general by 1692. He became a field marshal in 1702, by which time he had had a successful career as commander-in-chief in Ireland where he defeated the Jacobites at Aughrim. He later served in Flanders (1692–7), where he commanded the cavalry.

GOOR, Johan van (?), Dutch
A senior artillery officer who commanded the trayne of artillery in England in 1688. He was promoted to lieutenant-colonel in 1690 and to colonel in 1695, by which time he had taken charge of the artillery in Flanders. By 1701 he was a major-general.

s'GRAVENMOER, Adam van der Duyn, Heer van (1639–1693), Dutch
A colonel in 1668 he was, by 1674, quartermaster of Dutch cavalry and four years later quartermaster-general of the Dutch Army with the rank of major-general. He was appointed governor of Bergen-op-Zoom in 1690 and two years later promoted to lieutenant-general.

HESSE-KASSEL, Karl, Landgrave of (1654–1730), German
Major supporter of William III, supplying considerable numbers of subsidy troops.

HOLSTEIN-PLON, Jan Adolf, Duke of (1634–1704), German
Fought al Seneffe (1674) as a regimental commander. Governor of Maastricht in 1693 and made 1st field marshal of the Dutch Army the same year. He was captured at Huy in 1694.

HORNES, Willem Adriaan, Graf van (d.1694), Dutch
A close and trusted associate of King William, he was master-general of the Dutch artillery between 1672 and 1694.

d'HUYBERT, Johann (d.1701), Dutch
A major-general in 1694, he was promoted to lieutenant-general three years later.

d'IVOY, Fredrik Thomas van Hangest-Genlis (1663–1727), Dutch
A colonel from 1699, he was quartermaster-general of the Dutch Army in 1701.

LEINSTER, Meinhard von Schomberg, 1st Duke of (1641–1719), German
Eldest son of Wiliiam's great old general, he fought with a British brigade in Portugal between 1662 and 1668, and later (1686) against the Turks in the Emperor's service. A strong supporter of William of Orange, he was general of horse in England and played a decisive part in the Williamite victory at the Boyne. In 1692 he was created Earl of Leinster in the Irish peerage, and was commander-in-chief in England until 1697. He later served the Anglo-Dutch cause during the War of the Spanish Succession.

LIPPE, Frederik Adolf Graf von der (d.1718), German
Colonel in the Dutch Army from 1689, whilst ruling prince of Lippe.

NASSAU-SAARBRUCKEN, Walrad Count van (?), Dutch
Another cousin of William III, he was the 2nd Field Marshal of the Dutch Army from 1689 and then 1st Field Marshal after 1696.

OPDAM, Jacob van Wassenaer, Heer van (1635–1714), Dutch
A major-general in 1683, he was promoted to lieutenant-general in 1691 and to general at the beginning of the War of the Spanish Succession, however he was badly beaten in 1703 at Eckeren in one of the first engagements of the war, and shortly after retired from the army.

OVERKIRK, Henrik van Nassau, Heer van (1640–1708), Dutch
A further cousin of William III he was a major-general in 1683 and a lieutenant-general in English service from 1689 till 1691 when he transferred back with the same rank to the Dutch Army. A full general in 1701 be was also a courtier and master of the horse to William at the time of the King's death.

PORTLAND, Hans Willem Bentinck, 1st Earl of (1649–1709) Dutch
Lifelong friend, councillor and possibly lover to William of Orange. Until the rise of Albemarle (q.v.) the most important man at the King's court, being

both 1st Gentleman of the Bedchamber and a Privy Councillor. He was colonel of 'the Blues', who were also known at this time as Lord Portland's Horse. He was a major-general in the Dutch Army in 1683 and a lieutenant-general by 1691.

PUY, Louis Charles du (d? 1695), Dutch
Director-General of Dutch fortifications, 1692 to 1695.

RUVIGNY, Henri de Massue, Earl of Galway (1648–1720), French
A Huguenot, he served under Turenne 1672–5 before sailing to England after the Edict of Nantes had been revoked, where he became a major-general in 1691 and followed Ginkel (q.v.) as commander-in-chief in Ireland. Created Earl of Galway at the end of the Nine Years' War, he served in Spain and Portugal during the succession war but was badly defeated at Almanza (1707) by the Duke of Berwick in the most important engagement of the war in Spain. This battle ironically had a French army led by a Englishman (Berwick was an illegitimate son of James II) defeating an English (actually Anglo-Dutch, Spanish and Portuguese) army led by a Frenchman.

SALISCH, Ernst Willem van (?), Dutch
Major-general in 1694 and lieutenant-general in 1697, he was a full general in 1705.

SCHOMBERG, Herman van, 1st Duke of (1615–90), German
A Protestant born at Heidelberg in the Rhineland Palatinate he fought from 1633 in the Dutch, Swedish (1634), French (1635), Dutch (1639–50) and French again (1655–85) armies. During the latter period he commanded an Anglo-French force in Portugal (1661–8), a British force on an attack at Walcheren and finally was placed in command of the French army in Roussillon (1673–4). He rose through the ranks until, in 1675, he was made a Marshal of France. He quit the armies of the Sun King following the revocation of the Edict of Nantes, which Henri IV had set up to guarantee Protestants freedom to practice their religion. Firstly entering Brandenburg service he was then appointed second in command of the Williamite forces for the invasion of England. Commanding the British corps in Ireland he was criticised for the state of the army after its first winter there. However this was probably due to the poor training and experience of the British soldiers than any fault on Schomberg's part. Despite this it does seem to have cost him William's confidence. He led the first waves of troops across the ford at the Boyne, but was shot dead on reaching the far bank.

SLANGENBURG, Frederik van Baer (d.1713), Dutch
Major-general in 1683, and lieutenant-general in 1692.

SOLMS, Henrik Trajectinus, Graaf van (d.1693), Dutch
A lieutenant-general in 1683 and full general in 1691, he was one of King William's favourite officers. He commanded the *Garde* te Voet (Foot Guards) through the major engagements of the Nine Years' War but was generally

detested by the British officers and men for his arrogance and for having been thought responsible for the failure to support the British infantry at Steenkirk. He was therefore not missed following his death at Neerwinden in 1693.

SUZANNET, Frederic Henri, Marquis de la Forest (d.1710), French
A Huguenot friend of Schomberg (q-v.) he left the French army to join the Danish service after 1683. Served as major-general of Danish horse in Ireland 1691, and in 1694 lieutenant-general of Danish horse in Flanders.

TETTAU, Julius Ernst von (1644–1711), German
An East Prussian by birth he joined the Danish Army in 1657, transferring to the French three years later. He spent a period in the Brandenburg Army before rejoining the Danes as a colonel in 1676. He was a major-general by 1684 and served on Württemberg's staff in Ireland in 1690. King William had him appointed a Dutch lieutenant-general in 1696, but he retired to his estates in Prussia the following year.

TILLY, Albert-Octave, Comte T'Serclaes de (1646–1715), Walloon
A grandson of the famous Thirty Years' War general. In Spanish service from 1665–89 when he became commander of the army of the city of Liege with the Dutch rank of lieutenant-general.

TILLY, Claude Frederic, Comte T'Serclaes de (1651-1723), Walloon
Brother of Albert-Octave Tilly. After initial service in the Spanish army joined the Dutch in 1675, as a major. Latterly became colonel of horse (1680), major-general (1691) and lieutenant-general of horse (1695).

WALDECK, Georg Friedrich, Graf von (1620–1692), German
After serving in various German armies he entered Dutch service in 1672. He was promoted to 1st field marshal shortly after joining. He took part in the relief of Vienna in 1683 and followed this by serving the Emperor as a field marshal during the Hungarian campaigns of 1683 to 1685. Returning to Dutch service he commanded the allied armies in the Low Countries while William was tied up in England and Ireland. However, never a dynamic field commander, he was now a rather spent force and the alliance fared better after William returned to command.

WEIJBNOM, Johann Theobald van (1610–91), Dutch
Major-general in 1675 and lieutenant-general in 1683.

WIJNBERGEN, Ditmar van (d.1696), Dutch
Colonel in 1678 and a major-general in 1691, he was governor of Bergen-op-Zoom in 1694.

WÜRTTEMBERG-NEUSTADT, Ferdinand Wilhelm, Duke of (1659–1701), German
Served in army of Württemberg before transferring to Danish service. Went to the relief of Vienna in 1683 and later served in Hungary. Returned to

the Danish Army in 1686 and went on to serve as commander-in-chief of the Danish contingent in Ireland. Between 1691 and the end of the war commanded the Danish troops in Flanders. Served against the Swedes during the opening phase of the Great Northern War, but died in 1701 from complications from a wound suffered in 1685.

ZUYLESTEIN, Willem van Nassau, Heer van (1649–1716), Dutch
Another Nassau cousin of the King. A major-general in 1691, and a lieutenant-general in English Service, he was master of the robes and was created Earl of Rochford in 1695.

Plate Commentaries

Chapter 2, Part 1

Plate 1: The Dutch *Garde te Voet* 1688–1702
A. Musketeer, *Garde te Voet*, from around the end of the Nine Years' War. This is based on a modern reconstruction and shows the current Dutch thinking on the dress of William of Orange's Blue Guards. One of the most obvious features is the scruffy appearance of the soldier, which seems to be standard for all Dutch soldiers, both horse and foot. Certainly a lack of uniformity in, for example, headgear, with hats of various sizes and colours being worn. Crossbelts are notable even at this late date.
B. Musketeer 1691. Based on illustrations of Dutch Foot Guards by C.C.P. Lawson. Lawson was of the opinion that the Blue Guards of this period carried a collar of charges. However, as discussed above, this is a very questionable conclusion.
C. Officer, after Romeyn de Hooghe, *c.*1688–90
D. Sergeant, after Romeyn de Hooghe *c.*1688–90. Di shows the decorated sleeve shown on the painting of William's arrival in Torbay, a similar type of decoration is shown, in the same picture, on an officer in the foreground.
E. Grenadier, after Romeyn de Hooghe (all these de Hooghe illustrations are taken from engravings of William and his Guards). The picture shows the Grenadier cap as shown by Knotel in his famous plate of the regiment Friesheim and repeated in Barthorp and McBride's MA title on Marlborough's Army. It is noticeable that a number of de Hooghe's illustrations (as well as the painting of the landing at Torbay) show what appears to be a sash tied around the soldier's waist. The black and white plate shows the grenadier cap again along with a fur cap which may have been worn by the *Garde te Voet* during Marlborough's Wars.
F. Dutch officer in a painting by Mathijs Naiveu. Interesting braiding to the edge of hat and a 'Steenkirk' cravat.
G. *Garde te Voet* during Marlborough's Wars. Unbraided tricorn and red cravat. *c.*1706.

Plate 2
A. Colour constructed by Alan Sapherson from the above extracts from the

Wardrobe accounts. This bears little or no resemblance to any other colour carried by a Dutch infantry regiment. It seems likely that this is a misreading of the desciption and that the cross of St. George refers to the cross within the garter not a cross overall, as shown here.

B. The colour of the regiment after its period in English service, i.e. after 1697.

C. A Dutch colour after C.C.P. Lawson, this shows some of the features described in the Wardrobe account and may be a colour of the *Garde te Voet*.

D. and E. Two colours captured by the French during the War of the Austrian Succession (*c*.1746) showing the development of the regiment's colours during the eighteenth century.

F. St. George Cross and Garter, close up of the central feature of the colour.

G. As above with the addition of the Garter star.

H. The illustration of the colour shown in Romeyn de Hooghe which clearly shows some of the details mentioned in the Wardrobe accounts. However no trophies of arms can be seen and generally the colour resembles the Friesheim regimental colour (see J).

J. Colour of the Regiment Friesheim, after Knotel.

K. Dress of the regiment.

L. Officer, Torbay painting, see comments above regarding braided sleeves.

M. Sergeant, as above.

N. Colour of the *Garde te Voet c*.1780 shows a possible layout for the trophies of war, described in the wardrobe accounts.

Chapter 2, Part 2

The plates cover the information I have on Dutch infantry for this period. In only about 20 percent of the cases are the flags known, but in about 75 percent of the regiments something is known of their uniforms, although this is rarely complete and sometimes contradictory. The primary sources for this information are the lists compiled by officers serving in the allied army while the army was in camp. At Tilroy camp in 1690 and Gerpines in 1691 these details were collated. The information is only accurate for these two dates as new coats were issued every two years and the availability of material was always a more important criterion than consistency when purchasing new uniforms. Two other secondary sources are the excellent studies by Jean Belaubre of the allied armies and the Wagner and Goldburg cards which relate to the War of the Spanish Succession and are, in general, a slightly less reliable source. The best of the numerous other sources are listed in the bibliography.

Plate 3

A. Musketeer regiment von BIRKENFELD. Based on the Royal Collection watercolour, this illustration shows the elements of dress discussed before. The soldiers have usually been described as Dutch, but until recently I wasn't entirely convinced. However on close examination of the marks shown on the cartouche I believe them to be a version of the arms of Amsterdam (see Ai) probably a munition mark placed on equipment supplied by the city. This opens up the possibility of identifying the regiments in question, as they would need to have been maintained by Holland. The colours worn match those of Waldeck (5), Schimmelpenninck (26), Weede (27), Heyden (39), Protr (44) and Linstau (45). Of these Waldeck (1672–93) is the only unit maintained by Holland.

However, as it is impossible to align the date of a unit's issue of clothing with an approximation of the date of the picture, this is a rather fruitless pursuit. It could also be that the reason these soldiers' equipment is marked with the arms of Amsterdam rather than Holland is that they are civic guards or militia!

B. Grenadier of the Regiment Friesheim, after Knotel. Based on the grenadiers in the aforementioned de Hooghe print. This regiment is sometimes listed as fusiliers, so all may have worn the cap. It seems unlikely at any standardisation of grenadiers' caps was taking place at this time given the numerous different examples both extant and illustrated. If Knotel's attribution to Friesheim is wrong than that type may be specific to the *Garde te Voet*.

C. Grenadier cap from B.

D. Arms of the states of the Netherlands. Regularly depicted on the flags of the regiments they maintained.

E. Officer from the de Hooghe plate of the *Garde*/Friesheim regiment.
Unusually dressed officer who appears to be wearing some form of overcoat, this may be a 'watch coat' of the sort issued to soldiers when on sentry duty. There is an illustration of a Bavarian version in the 'Blauen Konig' series of plates by Hoffman.

F. The headgear of the soldiers in the picture in the Royal Collection. Two (figures F-iii and F-iv) appear to be Grenadiers with F-iv's not unlike those worn by British grenadiers from their earliest formation. F-ii's hat appears very stiff and may be made of leather, a hat not unlike this one is depicted in various paintings by Jan van Wyck, often on officers. Incidentally the works of van Wyck seem to support the slightly untidy look for Dutch infantry as in his pictures they also seem to be wearing hats of various different shades of brown and grey as well as black. The Royal Collection picture is in black and white in Osprey Men at Arms 267 *The British Army* by John Tincey and two of them are shown in colour in the Royal Collection catalogue.

G. Grenadier cap, Scots regiment Ponmore. Although the regiment in question falls outside the scope of this article, the cap shows another variant in existence.

H. A cap illustrated by Sapherson from an extant original, of which I have a black and white illustration. Shown for the same reason as G.

I. Grenadier cap Oranje-Friesland regiment.

Plate 4
Diagonal hatching shows that information is not available on this area.
(1) BULOW/WELDEREN from Tilroy and Wagner. Unusually NCOs wear silver lace and officers gold. Colonel;s colour would have a white field and possibly arms of Gelderland (Dvii) in the corner.
(2) WUNBERGEN/BEIJNHEIM from Tilroy, Gerpines, Wagner and Belaubre. Gerpines says green linings, the rest red. Maybe an error or just a change of coat. Colour shown colonel's: others have yellow field.
(3) ESSEN/PLATTENBURG

(4) *Garde te Voet*

(5) WALDECK/HOLSTEIN-PLON red coat from Tilroy and Gerpines. Grey coat from 1700.

(6) HORNES-KASSEL/ST. AMANT from Belaubre, earlier coat colours from 1674 also shown.

(7) DELWICH/LINDEBOOM from Belaubre for 1689 issue. Grey coat from Gerpines 1691.

(8) BIRKENFELD (see Plate 3).

(10) BEAUMONT/COEHOORN, red coat from Tilroy, grey from Wagner. Colour shown colonel's; others have yellow field.

(11) TASSIN DE TORSAY, earlier 1680 blue coat from Belaubre, red from Gerpines.

(12) PERCEVAL/SWANSBEL Belaubre.

(13) ZOBEL/GOOR – green lining Gerpines, red and drummer Belaubre from 1701.

(14) SALISCH from Tilroy, Gerpines and Wagner. Colonel's colour has white field.

(15) FAGEL from Tilroy, Gerpines and Belaubre. Ribbons on both shoulders.

(16) HORNES-BOXTEL/SOUTELANDE Gerpines.

(17) SLANGENBURG from Tilroy, Gerpines and Wagner. Colonel's colour white field.

(19) VAN SAIM/DOHNA from Tilroy and Belaubre blue lining, Gerpines white.

Plate 5

(18) BRANDENBURG, colonel's colour shown, field for others unknown.

(20) L'ECLUSE/NASSAU WALLOONS from Gerpines, Wagner and Belaubre. Colonel's colour field white.

(21) LANNOY VAN DER MEULEN/HOLSTEIN-NORBURG from Belaubre. Men had aiguillettes, colour unknown.

(22) AMELISWEERD from Tilroy and Belaubre.

(23) NASSAU SAARBRUCKEN/VAN DER BEKE, red lining from Wagner, blue from a list of deserters 1689.

(24) NOYELLES Gerpines.

(26) SCHIMMELPENNINCK/ARENTS/VASSY Gerpines.

(27) WEEDE/NASSAU-WOUDENBURG, all sources contradict on this one, probably all red with blue lining to late 1690s, then grey.

(28) VAN HAGEDOORN/MARQUETTE/PALLANDT from Wagner, field of colonel's colour white.

(29) LÜNEBURG-OSNABRUCK/FRIESEN/TETTAU/KEPPEL, grey coat from Gerpines, red from Belaubre.

(30) HAERSOLTE/SALM/RANCK from Tilroy and Belaubre.

(31) DU THEIL/WAES from Geprpnes and Wagner. Colonel's colour white with the same corner decoraion, arms of Utrecht top left corner, gold wreath, arm and cloud as 28. Gold motto 'HAEC LIBERTATIS ERGO'.

(33) NASSAU/ORANJE (FRIESLAND) from Tilroy, Gerpines and Wagner. Colonel's colour the same with arms illustrated in the top left corner.

(34) AYLVA/SCHRATENBACH from Tilroy.

(36) SCHELTINGA/VEGELIN from Belaubre. Sergeants in reverse colours,

Plate 1

The Dutch *Garde te Voet* 1688–1702

(Illustration by Mark Allen © Wargames Illustrated)

See main text for further information.

Plate 2

Colours of the *Garde te Voet*
(Illustration by Mark Allen © Wargames Illustrated)
See main text for further information.

ii

Dutch Grenadiers
(Illustration by Mark Allen © Wargames Illustrated)
See main text for further information.

iii

Plate 4

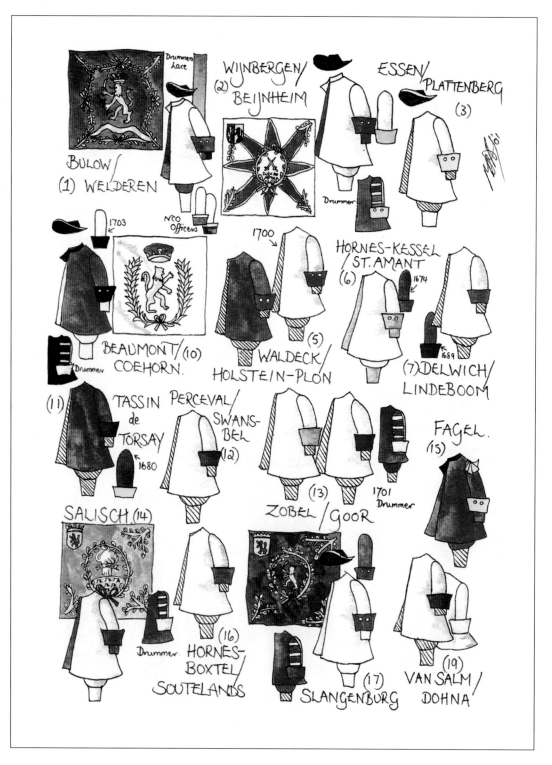

Dutch Regiments of Foot
(Illustration by Mark Allen © Wargames Illustrated)
See main text for further information.

Plate 5

Dutch Regiments of Foot

(Illustration by Mark Allen © Wargames Illustrated)

See main text for further information.

Plate 6

The *Garde du Corps* (after Romeyn de Hooghe)
(Illustration by Mark Allen © Wargames Illustrated)
See main text for further information.

Plate 7

Dutch Cavalry Types 1680–1695 (after de Hooghe etc.)
(Illustration by Mark Allen © Wargames Illustrated)
See main text for further information.

 # Plate 8

Dutch Cavalry Regiments
(Illustration by Mark Allen © Wargames Illustrated)
See main text for further information.

Plate 9

Dutch Dragoons 1688–1702
(Illustration by Mark Allen © Wargames Illustrated)
See main text for further information.

ix

Plate 10

Dutch Artillery 1688–1702
(Illustration by Mark Allen © Wargames Illustrated)
See main text for further information.

Plate 11

William III, His Allies and Generals
(Illustration by Mark Allen © Wargames Illustrated)
See main text for further information.

Plate 12

Maximilian Emmanuel, Elector of Bavaria
(Illustration by Mark Allen © Wargames Illustrated)
See main text for further information.

Plate 13

William III's Dutch and German Generals
(Illustration by Mark Allen © Wargames Illustrated)
See main text for further information.

Plate 14

Outline of British Military Dress 1660–1702

(Illustration by Mark Allen © Wargames Illustrated)

See main text for further information.

Plate 15

Outline of British Military Dress 1660–1702

(Illustration by Mark Allen © Wargames Illustrated)

See main text for further information.

Plate 16

British Regiments, 1685–1702
(Illustration by Mark Allen © Wargames Illustrated)
See main text for further information.

Plate 17

British Regiments, 1685–1702

(Illustration by Mark Allen © Wargames Illustrated)

See main text for further information.

Plate 18

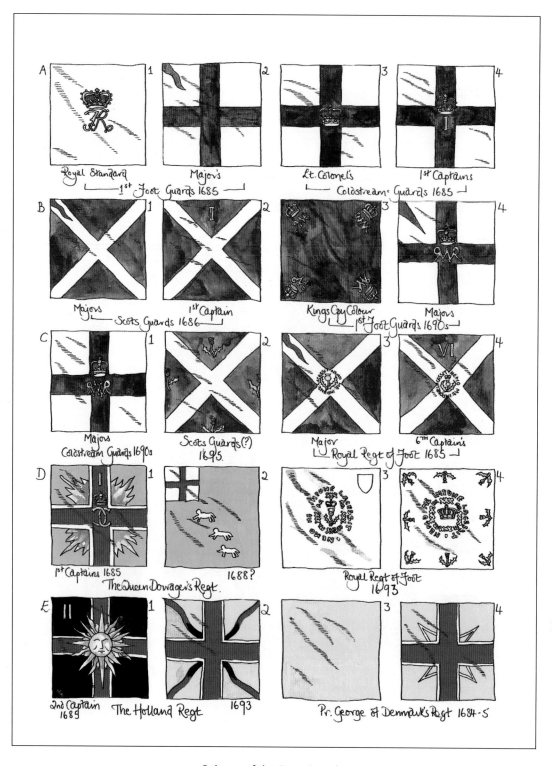

Colours of the Foot Guards

(Illustration by Mark Allen © Wargames Illustrated)

See main text for further information.

Plate 19

Line Regiments' Colours

(Illustration by Mark Allen © Wargames Illustrated)

See main text for further information.

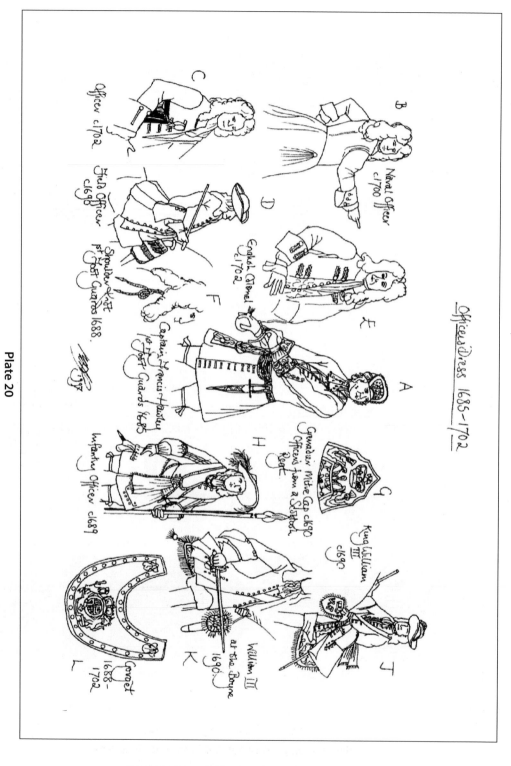

Plate 20

Officers' Dress 1685–1702

(Illustration by Mark Allen © Wargames Illustrated)

See main text for further information.

Officers' Clothing 1685–1702

(Illustration by Mark Allen © Wargames Illustrated)

See main text for further information.

Plate 21

Soldiers of the Gardes Françaises, c.1696 (after Giffart)

(Illustration by Mark Allen © Wargames Illustrated)

See main text for further information.

Plate 22

Officer, Garde Française
c.1703

Drummer, Garde Française
c.1740

Sargeant's
Partizan
c.1707

Garde Française 1710

Colours and clothing of the *Gardes Françaises*, 1703–1710
(Illustration by Mark Allen © Wargames Illustrated)
See main text for further information.

Plate 23

Pikeman, Gardes Suisses 1690

Gardes Suisses c.1710.

Officer, Gardes Suisse .1710

Colours and Clothing of the *Gardes Suisse*
Illustration by Mark Allen © Wargames Illustrated
See main text for further information.

silver lace. Officers red coat, gold lace.

(37) LIMBURG-STYRUM/COEHORN from Belaubre.

(39) COEVERDEN/HEYDEN from Tilroy and Belaubre, officers in red

(43) STADHOUDER GRONINGEN

(44) PROTT from Belaubre. Sergeants crimson cuffs. Officers red.

(45) LINSTAU from Belaubre.

(49) HEECKEREN/ELS from Belaubre. Ribbons on the right shoulder only.

(51) GOES/HOLSTEIN-BECK from Tilroy and Belaubre

Note: There are a small number of unidentified flags, plus some which date from the eighteenth century and which may be relevant. These will all be illustrated below.

Chapter 2, Part 3: Guard and Line Cavalry

Plate 6: *Garde du Corps* and *Gardes te Paard*

A, B, C, D and F show the dress of the *Garde du Corps* van Zijne Majesteit and E, G, H, I, J, K and L the dress of the *Gardes te Paard* based on written descriptions and the plates of artists such as Romeyn de Hooghe and Jan Wyck. Both the *Garde du Corps* and the *Garde te Paard* appear to have worn coats with hanging sleeves. However although the colours of the top coats have been described in written sources, the under coat has not. The choices are probably between a leather or material vest (waistcoat) with sleeves (or less probably without) or another coat of similar style, but possibly of thinner material, to the top coat. As the regiments were brigaded together and in style were dressed pretty much the same, the line illustrations of de Hooghe are not very helpful in telling them apart.

A. Trooper *Garde du Corps* showing the leather type vest as described above.

B. Officer of the *Garde du Corps* wearing armour and with a coat decorated in gold lace. Like the troopers of the the regiment, officers rode greys. His sash is blue.

C. Shabraque for the *Garde du Corps*.

D. Standard of the *Garde du Corps*. Sapherson describes the *Garde du Corps* as decorated with the monogram of William and Mary and the *Gardes te Paard* with just William's. However it may be that the *Gardes te Paard* was a later issue, post-dating Queen Mary's death in 1694. The fringes of the *Garde du Corps* standard are a mix of gold and silver.

E. Trumpeter of *Gardes te Paard* based on a de Hooghe plate. The arms on the sleeve may be those of England.

F. Trumpeter of the *Garde du Corps* after a hand-coloured version of a de Hooghe plate, the colours may be dubious, but they are reasonably close to the written descriptions we have available.

G. Standard of the *Gardes te Paard*, see comments at D above.

H. to L. Various illustrations of *Gardes te Paard* troopers taken from de Hooghe's version of the battle of the Boyne. The monogram on the sleeve seems to have been the major difference visible on the line drawing, however it might be the case that both regiments wore it!

Plate 7: Dutch Cavalry Types 1680–1695. After de Hooghe
This plate attempts to show some genetic styles in dress of Dutch cavalry. Most of the figures (excluding I and J) were based on line drawings and therefore the colours are speculative.

A. Dutch cavalry officer's hat 1688.
B. Hat similar to those worn by Croat light cavalry shown on a Dutch or Danish cavalryman *c*.1688.
C. See B.
D. From a painting by Jan Wyck. may be a *Garde du Corps* trooper (see also D1).
E. After de Hooghe *c*.1688.
F. and G. From de Hooghe engraving of the Boyne.
H. As F. and G.
I. After Jan Wyck. 1690s. From a Huytenburgh painting of the siege of Namur.

Plate 8
(1) Flag on the right is the colonel's standard. Tilroy shows white lined red and Jean Belaubre has the trumpeters in red. But both Gerpines and Wagner have the linings in blue and the latter shows buff waistcoats and breeches! Note: on the plate the pistol holsters (after Tilroy) should also be red).
(3) This is is after the Tilroy reference. Gerpines shows white lined red. Officers may have worn green, lined crimson.
(9) Tilroy red coat, lined in red. Wagner shows pink facings
(10) Gerpines and Wagner agree on the facings, but both Wagner and Belaubre say the coat was a darker grey. The shabraque was red laced white. The white flag is the regimental or colonel's standard, the other the squadron. Gerpines says white, lined red. Belaubre, by 1695 – it was white, lined white(18) Gerpines white, lined green. Belaubre, for 1692 grey, lined red. The grey may have been dark.
(20) Red facings (Gerpines); 1692 blue facings. Belaubre believes that by 1695 the facings were red again.
(21) After Wagner. The standard shown is the regimental, the squadron ones were straw coloured.
(23) After Gerpines and Wagner.
(28) Tilroy shows white, lined red; Gerpines white, lined blue. After Gerpines. The cap is speculative and is based on a painting by Huytenburgh.

Part 4: Dragoons and Artillery

Plate 9: Dutch Dragoons 1688–1702
Eppinger's Dragoons wore a darkish grey coat, lined in black. A grey fur cap with a brown bag., probably laced silver or white. Officers wore black hats laced silver and musicians' (normally drummers and hautbois in dragoon regiments) coats were also laced silver. Shabraques were probably black laced

white or silver.. Contemporary paintings seem to show vest (waistcoat) and breeches in buff (leather?) but this cannot be confirmed. The regimental standard may have been carried by the first company with the others carrying guidons (certainly this is the rank list for the regimental standard bearers in contemporary sources). The standards and guidons may also have carried Queen Mary's monogram prior to her death in 1694. There is also some evidence from some sources that the flags were plain black!

Tilroy shows Maritza in red coats lined white, while Belaubre list red coats lined in blue. The Guidon is for Dopoff.

Plate 10: Dutch Artillery 1688–1702

There are two possible uniforms for the artillery. One is blue faced red, and the other is blue faced orange which was supplied to the English 'trayne' for service in Ireland. This is usually described as being done to honour William, but may also have been done as a Dutch artillery uniforms were available. Also the references to Dutch artillery in blue faced red date mainly from the eighteenth century when the role of the Stadtholder was lesss esteemed and the Foot Guards were also changing from orange to red facings.

The small figures at the bottom of the plate are copied from various versions of Jan Wyck's painting of the Boyne. In the same group of paintings it would seem that Dutch ordinance was painted grey.

Part 5: William's Allies and Generals

Plate 11: William III His Allies and Generals

A. From a follower of Jan Wyck, the original has a depiction of the Battle of the Boyne. Like some other more naive treatments this may be a truer example of William in the field than some more polished observations.
B. Again by a follower of Wyck, this is a very typical design of the period, see Plate 13C for another example. Unlikely to be an authentic record, William would be unlikely to wear armour.
C. Copy of a studio portrait, possibly the suit was one owned by the King.
D. Small figure in a large picture by Storek of William about to set sail for England. Unlikely to be an accurate representation, in the original the likeness isn't very good either.
E. Good studio portrait by Jan Wyck, plus many copies by other hands. Background shows William III's arrival in England so this may have been the suit he wore on that occasion.
F. Another Boyne image, possibly by Wyck. Likely to be based on clothing worn by William, however probably not that which he wore at the Boyne.
G. From a large view of the Battle of the Boyne. Probably an accurate depiction of King William in grey.
H. As G.

Plate 12: Elector Maximilian Emmanuel of Bavaria. Ally of William III until 1702, and Louis XIV thereafter (1662–1726)

A. From a portrait of the Elector dating from the 1680s.

B. Portrait of Max Emmanuel following his successful involvement in the campaign to relieve Vienna in 1683.

C. This is taken from a famous depiction of the relief of Vienna, 1683. The Elector can be seen leading the Bavarian contingent against the Turks.

D. A later studio portrait from around the turn of the century.

E. From Hoffmann's series of plates on the Bavarian army. The plate dates from the early years of the twentieth century.

F. A much later portrait of the Elector, in hunting garb.

Plate 13: William III's Dutch and German Generals

A. Bentinck appears here in the uniform of his cavalry regiment (later the Royal Horse Guards).

B. A German ally in ceremonial dress wearing the order of the 'Golden Fleece'. This was an award given by the Habsburgs to their supporters.

C. A studio portrait from the same design as the earlier depiction of King William in Plate 11. The armour was certainly never worn in the field.

D. Schomberg's son from another studio portrait.

E. Two paintings of the great engineer with a period of 30 years in between.

F. Another studio portrait of the King, comments in 11C are probably true for this picture too.

G. The King's old general shown during the late 1680s.

H. Probably dating from after his service in the Nine Years' War but before his involvement in the Spanish Succession conflict.

I. The victor of the war in Ireland, as seen in a studio portrait from the late 1690s. Earlier comments on the wearing of armour hold true here as well.

J. A later colouring of a contemporary plate showing Ellenburg in his pomp as well as a depiction of his execution, which if accurately shown, was achieved with a sword and with the victim kneeling up.

3

The British Army

The objective of this chapter is to present a detailed series of plates illustrating the dress of the British Army during the formative years between the restoration of King Charles II and the reign of Queen Anne. I hope there will be some 'groundbreaking' information and reconstructions, however the majority of the emphasis of this series will be on bringing together research from many different primary and secondary sources and illustrating this work in a convenient way for students of military history and for wargamers.

Part One: An Outline of Military Dress 1660–1702

During the period we are considering, tremendous changes took place in the social and political structure of this country and these changes seem to have been reflected in the clothing people wore. There came to an end the centuries-old ensemble of doublet and breeches and the introduction of the coat and waistcoat (known hereafter by its correct seventeenth century name of vest).

Britain generally followed French fashion, with variations due to a certain conservatism in matters of taste. France had, since the 1630s, been the leading Western European nation in most cultural fields, following the decline and stagnation of Spain, and this was accelerated by the ambition of her dynamic young king, Louis XIV.

As an outline of how military dress developed I intend to look at each decade in turn.

The 1660s

Soldiers were still dressed, for the most part, in doublet and breeches at the beginning of the decade, although the doublet was beginning to be replaced by the cassock, which had previously been worn over the doublet as bad weather protection. There is some evidence that even during the early years of the Thirty Years' War the garment issued as regimental uniform was in fact the cassock. However by the 1660s the cassock may have been more like a longer version of the soldier's coat of the Civil War period (see Plate 14, G) than the cumbersome overcoat of the early 1620s.

The hat was probably not yet of a uniform style, colour or size, but grey, black and brown were the most likely colours. The Swedish army had standardised the issue of grey hats to most infantry regiments by the middle of the previous decade, but in the British army there was either no standard issue or it was left to the discretion of the regimental colonel.

The 1670s

By the late 1660s the long coat, of French origin, had been introduced to the army, together with uniformity of headgear. The latter were usually black for the infantryman with a taped edge in yellow or white.

Officers adopted the coat with sleeves turned back to the elbow, and where a vest was worn this was also sleeved, the sleeves being exposed below the cuff of the coat. Hats for officers at first became small and uniform, like the men's, but as the decade went on became larger and larger. However grey was the only colour besides black to be popular. Some cavalry regiments were issued grey rather than black hats, but most still campaigned in the ubiquitous 'lobster pot' helmet (see Plate 14, E and M). Stockings became issue garments and over-hose were no longer worn (compare Plate 14, G and J). Shoes became uniformly black.

During 1677 and 1678 both the Guards and the line regiments were allowed to raise grenadier companies (see Plate 14, L).

The 1680s

The standardisation continued as equipment became more uniform with waist belts replacing baldricks as the accepted method of carrying the sword. By the middle of the decade the plug bayonet was beginning to be introduced and towards the end of the 1680s the cartridge box was replacing the bandoliers. Grenadier caps were now as likely to be of a material construction than of fur and were often decorated with the sovereign's initials.

The cut of officers' coats became more closely shaped, with the sleeves becoming longer and tighter fitting (see Plate 15, L). The hat still retained its size, although colours other than black were now unusual. Officers' hats were usually edged with gold or silver lace, depending on their regiment's button colour, although officers made little other concession to regimental uniformity.

1690s

Cartridge boxes became the norm in infantry battalions and rank and file hats began to take on the tricorn shape which would dominate the next century. Officers' coats became more shapely and vents and pleats became more fashionable (see Plate 15, T). Breeches were cut less generously than was popular during the 70s and 80s. Sashes were worn higher and were often tied at the front of the waist (compare Plate 15, L, with D). Like the common soldiery, officers' hats began to be turned up like the later tricorns, however feathers were not abandoned until the next century had begun.

Wigs

The periwig or peruke was an important part of a gentleman's apparel from the early 1660s onwards. At first it was a concession to the impracticalities of the long hair fashionable at the time, but later became a fashion accessory in its own right. The shape of periwigs reflected this change, with those of the 1660s attempting to produce the look of real hair and later models becoming more unnatural. Generally wigs became larger and taller and by the early 1690s often had pointed horns or other exaggerations protruding from the top. Likewise colours became more unusual with reddy browns, greys (often with bizarre tinges of colour), and (later) whites popular.

Plates 14 and 15: An Outline of Military Dress

Plate 14

A. Officer from an engraving of the funeral of the Duke of Albemarle 1670. In mourning costume with black ribbons, this officer is wearing a simpler version of **Plate 15, N**. Note that unlike the soft leather 'bucket tops' of the Civil War period the heavy 'jacked' boots worn at this time were not practical for dismounted duties.

B. Trooper of a regiment of horse during the 1690s. Images of British cavalrymen of this period are extremely rare, so this is a possible reconstruction. The cavalry had by this time given up their pot helmets, but to what extent body armour was worn is a matter of some conjecture. Certainly it had been discontinued by 1707, for in that year Marlborough reintroduced armour to his cavalry regiments serving in Flanders. However by 1707 the armour was worn beneath the coat. Whether this was the case in the 1690s is debatable.

C. Trooper of the Duke of York's Horse Guards from the Hollar engraving of Charles II's coronation. Wearing back- and breastplates and a buff-coat decorated with gold lace this gentleman trooper is a cut above the rank and file that made up the King's small standing army in 1660. The breeches are close to the proportions normally associated with a type known as 'petticoat' breeches, although this style was never adopted widely by soldiers due to its impracticality.

D. Cavalryman in the background of a portrait of the Duke of Monmouth, *c*.1672. The portrait appears to represent the Duke during his period as commander of the brigade of British troops in French service. The skirmish in the background shows both British and Dutch cavalry dressed in buff-coats, back- and breastplates and an assortment of hats and helmets.

E. English officer of horse *c*.1670. Reconstructed from the fashionable dress of the day and equipped with back- and breastplates and a pot helmet.

F. Pikeman of the Coldstream Regiment of Foot Guards *c*.1669.

F1. Alternative neckwear for E.

G. Reconstruction of a Foot Guards musketeer at the time of the Restoration in 1660. For many years the Dutch illustration of King Charles from Holland was thought to show the dress of the King's Regiment of Foot Guards. Although certain aspects of the dress are compatible with this assumption, the wearing of 'lobster pot' helmets by the figures in question makes this assumption doubtful. My belief is that they are possibly Dutch dragoons, although more research is necessary before a definite conclusion can be made.

H. General illustration of the dress of pikemen during the 1660s.

J. Musketeer *c*.1687. Equipped with a matchlock musket, bandoliers and a plug bayonet, this is the ideal of the well-armed musketeer which was the aim of most line regiments towards the end of James II's reign. The major changes in dress between this figure and **14, G** include: the lengthening of the coat, the size of the cuffs, new pockets and buttons and the uniformity of the hat. Only the introduction of the plug bayonet marks any major change in equipment.

J1. Rear view of **J.**

J2. Close-up of plug bayonet and sheath.

K. Musketeer of King William's army *c.*1694. The bandoliers have been replaced by an ammunition pouch or box and whilst this illustration represents (as **J**) a musketeer, a growing number of the King's soldiers were armed with flintlocks. Most pikemen were now unarmoured and their numbers had dropped to about 20 percent of a battalion's strength.

L. Introduced into the army during the late 1670s, the grenadier was armed with a bag of grenades (usually four) as well as a flintlock musket, plug bayonet and an axe. This one dates from 1686.

L. 1–4. Show alternative grenadier caps from the reign of James.

M. Trooper of a Scottish regiment of horse during the reign of James II. Modern reconstructions for the 'Scots Greys' dragoon regiment show members of said regiment wearing older style buff-coats over their uniform coats. This figure is an attempt to relate this to the dress of a regiment of horse. Note the continued use of both armour and the pot helmet.

The standard dress of the British soldier at the beginning of the wars of Queen Anne 1702. The hat has begun to he formalised into a tricorn of sorts and the soldier is equipped with ammunition box and flintlock.

N1. Two different styles of collar coming into vogue on soldiers' coats. These two are attributed to the Guards and dated 1704, however there is some evidence that coats of this type were not issued until some time later.

N2. The socket bayonet gradually issued to the British infantry during the early years of the eighteenth century.

Plate 15

A to K show the development of neckwear during the period. From the bands (collars) popular at the Restoration through to various styles of cravat, which were to dominate western dress for the next 200 years, in one form or another:

A. After Hollar's engraving of Charles II's Coronation. One of the King's Horse Guards. This picture shows the high crown hat, which had been popular for much of the previous decade, decorated with feathers and ribbons. This fashion would .soon be superseded by hats with smaller crowns and much larger brims (**K, L, N and R**). The figures wear a style of band described as bib, this was the 'swansong' of the falling collar prior to its replacement by the cravat. This bib band had developed from wider shallower styles which had been popular during the 1630s and 1640s but which had been replaced by smaller bands during the Commonwealth and Protectorate, Whilst the 'old chestnut' of 1650s England being full of sombre Puritans in plain white collars is not borne out by the surviving portraits, there does appear to have been a return to the more simple forms of neckwear.

However, with the return of the King the court proceeded to introduce the excess of French fashion, one of these being the bib band (called a rabat by the French). Although bands of this shape were worn in undecorated linen (see 15, B) the fashion item normally had a lawn inset surrounded with Venetian 'grospoint', or similar lace.

In Italy and France bands were sometimes constructed entirely of lace without any plain material, but this was uncommon in England. The band strings were usually long enough to protrude slightly beneath the bottom edge of the band and were normally large and heavily fringed. For a detailed examination of the dress normally associated with this hat and band see **Plate 14, C.**

B. A simple form of the band described above, worn with civilian clothing from 1667. At this time Charles II, hoping to break the dominance of the French court of Louis XIV, introduced a new costume to his court. Never seriously adopted by the military, it consisted of a long shapeless coat worn over a similarly styled vest (waistcoat). Louis countered all this by putting his liveried pages into this style, a considerable insult, and the fashion was withdrawn. The band itself was probably worn by many junior officers of inferior means unable to afford the more expensive lace bands.

C. James II as Duke of York, shortly after the restoration. The Duke wears an even larger band than in **A**. The difficulties of campaigning in this type of neckwear had been apparent during the wars earlier in the century, both in England and on the continent. Soldiers during the Civil War had often pulled the furthest corners of their bands around to the front and tied them together (with either coloured ribbons, the band strings or simply together). While another alternative was to replace the cumbersome band with a length of linen tied around the neck.

D. Originally worn by Croatian fight cavalry, the name cravat probably came from a French corruption of the German name for these Croat troops 'Crabatten'. Early examples of the cravat were often plain, however they soon came to be made of the same sorts of lace which had previously decorated the bib band. At this time they were held together with thin lengths of coloured ribbon.

E. Very similar to **D**. This is in fact a Dutch officer although Englishmen would be wearing cravats of this type.

F. In the next stage of its development the cravat was 'backed' by an array of stiffened ribbons, often in colours matching those decorating the coat, breeches or shoes. This type of cravat was worn by soldiers but had lost out by the late 1680s to the simpler style of **G**.

G. Portrait of Colonel Luttrell, colonel of a foot regiment (see section on the Army of William). Luttrell wears a simple cravat of Venetian lace unadorned by ribbons. As the 1690s progressed the ribbons became less and less common, dying out altogether with the advent of the 'Steenkirk'.

H. In 1692 during William III's surprise attack an the French encampment at Steenkirk the *Gardes Françaises* were unable to dress themselves in time to counter the Allied offensive, and fought in a half state. In this condition they managed to push back the repeated attacks by the British troops facing them and in the process created a new mode of dress. This new style involved the clothing being worn in a generally unkempt manner (often the coat would be worn without the vest, revealing the shirt beneath, this was thought particularly 'sexy'. In the case of the cravat, the style determined that it should be worn wrapped loosely around the neck, with the ends tucked into convenient buttonholes, to avoid it becoming unravelled.

I. Simple way of wearing the cravat on campaign, the ends were pushed down into the front of the coat after tying. Very suitable when wearing armour, the loose ends of the cravat being secure beneath the breastplate.

J. Method of pulling ends of cravat through buttonholes for 'Steenkirk' style of wear. Note: the ends have been knotted to make them more secure. This is 1704, and still popular in England, this style had died out much earlier in France.

K. Taken from a set of playing cards depicting Monmouth's Rebellion. A very plain hat adorned with a feather, shows less French influence than **L** or **N**. In France, and increasingly in England, the custom was growing to pull up the fronts, and often the backs, of hats. Ribbons as per **F**.

L. The coat has developed from **N** (see below) becoming longer and straighter. It has none of the gathers and vents which would appear later. The sleeves were very tight with the cuffs appearing much lower than had previously been the case. In England coats were more often of one colour than would have been the case in France, and less likely to have been heavily decorated in ribbons. Note how low the sash has been tied. The breeches are the last form to be unusual or distinctive before a much simpler style came in during the second half of the decade.

M. A typical method of campaigning would be to tie the wig at the back in a form of 'pony-tail'. This later developed into the 'bag-wig' style which would end the dominance of the full-bottomed wig.

N. There are a number of portraits of English officers at this time displaying all the requisites of high fashion in France. The Duke of Monmouth had led a brigade of British soldiers to the aid of Louis XlV in his war against the Dutch, and it is probably due to this that the following of French styles reached its apogee during the 1670s. The dress still has martial elements visible beneath all the foppery, with a leather buff vest, worn under the coat, being the most obvious example.

O. Taken from a portrait of the Duke of Monmouth with the sleeves of a buff vest showing below the cuffs of the coat. The vest is otherwise of the same cut as in **N**.

P. Colonel John Russell, colonel of the First Foot Guards at the Restoration. Showing the dress of a senior officer at the beginning of our period. Russell wears his buff coat over other items of dress, unlike the later developments (see **N and O** above). Alter the Civil War the length of the buff-coat increased, with the bottom edge of the tabs often falling on or below the tops of the new style of 'jacked' boot. With the decline of the doublet and its replacement with the coat and vest, the buff-coat took on the style and shape of the vest and was usually, thereafter, worn beneath the coat. In the illustration Russell has separate sleeves tied onto his buff-coat by means of arming or 'ribbonpoints' rather than a doublet worn underneath, which was another alternative.

Q. Sleeve of Colonel Legge from slightly later than **P**, shown to illustrate a different form of sleeve to be worn with a buff-coat as in **P**. Vertical decoration was becoming move popular than the horizontal type so common during the

Civil War. See also **Plate 14, C** and Sir Peter Lely's series of portraits of naval officers, dating to this period.

R. After Sir Godfrey Kneller's portrait of Captain Thomas Lucy of the Royal Regiment of Horse. Unusual to see the wearing of the buff-coat as an outer garment, this late. Certainly most of the rank and file of the regiment would have been wearing their coats over the top of buff vests. This may be an individual 'whim'. See Plate 14, C and E for further discussion of this topic, also Michael Basthorp's *British Cavalry Uniforms* for another version of the painting.

S. During the early years of this decade (1680s) there appeared a number of portraits of both British and continental officers wearing cloth coats coloured and cut as if made of buff, although usually heavily decorated. Most of the work in Britain was carried out by a French artist Henri Gascon. Whether these works depicted actual clothing or some classical image is difficult to tell however as the trend was fairly widespread it seemed a good idea to include it.

T. The standard dress of most British army officers of the 1690s. Although certain aspects changed during this time – sleeves widened, cuffs got bigger – this silhouette remains reasonably constant. Note that ribbons have by now almost disappeared from fashionable clothing.

U. Typical English style of coat decoration from the turn of the century.

V. Tighter breeches popular from the later 1680s. This pair have a roll to enable the stockings to be held tight and kept smooth, a fashionable necessity.

W. Cuff from the mid 1690s decorated in the French style. In England this would have been plainer. Note how far the sleeves of the vest extend below the coat.

X. Sleeve from the end of the period. The sleeve is now much wider and the cuff larger than before. Note how the vest sleeve (in yellow) is folded hack over the cuff, a common style until vests became sleeveless.

Part Two: The Infantry of James II and William III

The period 1685–1702 was one of profound change and upheaval in Britain, not only for the military, but also politically, economically and socially. Had the so called 'Glorious Revolution' not occurred in 1688 then the shape of British history could well have been very different. In 1685 that much overrated monarch Charles II died and left the throne to his brother James, who because of his Roman Catholicism had been subjected to various attempts to exclude him from the succession. His arrival on the throne was initially welcomed as he had behaved with great dignity throughout the period of the 'exclusion' bills and was popular in the country. He also cut a somewhat dashing figure as a man of action, having served in the 1650s both in the French army under Turenne (who had a high opinion of him) and later with the Royalist army in 'exile', allied to the Spanish, at the Battle of the [Dunkirk] Dunes (1658). After the Restoration he took responsibility for the navy, doing good service in correcting the many organisational faults as well fulfilling the role of admiral, with some successes, during the Dutch wars.

Unfortunately his reign as monarch was not as successful. Although he managed to weather the attempt by his nephew James, Duke of Monmouth, to usurp the throne, he failed to gauge the mood of the country and his policy of allowing toleration for Catholics and Protestant dissenters was seen as an attempt to re-Catholicise the nation. In Ireland the realities of these policies became transparent as his deputy the Earl of Tyrconnell purged the military establishment of its Protestant officers, replacing them with loyal Catholics.

In foreign policy James continued his brother's close ties with the France of Louis XIV, which was also unpopular in the country, particularly after the Revocation of the Edict of Nantes sent thousands of Protestant French families to seek asylum in Britain, bringing with them horror stories of life under the 'Sun King'. Indeed the foreign policy implications of James's closeness to King Louis were as important a factor as any in causing his demise.

James's daughter Mary was married to the Dutch Stadtholder William of Orange-Nassau, a figure of considerable importance on the European stage. William's Netherlands were the arch enemy of France and his fears for his country following an Anglo-French alliance led him to take drastic action to protect both the Netherlands and his wife's inheritance, the latter having been threatened by the birth of a son to James and his young Italian wife, Mary of Modena. The birth of the young James also threaten the future of the 'Protestant Succession': toleration could be given to one Catholic monarch, who could be treated as a 'blip' before normality was resumed, but a dynasty was a different matter!

William found himself forced to take action. He arranged for the army of Brandenburg to defend Holland whilst he gathered a small but well-trained army to invade England with the intention of forcing his uncle to change his policies. In the end the project worked better than planned, with James fleeing the country and William created dual monarch with his wife Mary. If the new king could gain the support of Parliament he would now be able to commit British soldiers to the coming war against France.

The British Army under James II and William III

James very rapidly increased the size of the standing army in Britain, much against the will of Parliament which feared he might use it to change the constitution in support of his co-religionists. During 1685–1688 he raised 18 battalions of foot, 14 regiments of horse and two of dragoons. All this while the country was ostensibly at peace. William of Orange continued this expansion, raising 66 battalions during 1688–1698. These were reduced by 51 at the end of the Nine Years' War (1688–97) and three more battalions were disbanded before 1714. However in readiness for the coming conflict over the Spanish Succession 20 battalions were raised between June 1701 and February 1702.

Organisation – the Infantry Battalion

During the reign of King James most regiments were formed with a single battalion organisation (only the First Foot Guards, the Scots Guards and the Royal Regiment had two). The battalion consisted of 13 companies, one of which was comprised of grenadiers. The grenadier company had no pikemen, but the remainder were made up of both pikemen and musketeers, with the former making up around a third of the company. By 1690 the proportions were around 5:1 in favour of the musketeers. In July 1685 the King reduced the strength of a company from approximately 111 men of all ranks to the following: 1 captain, 1 lieutenant, 1 ensign, 2 sergeants, 2 corporals, 2 drummers, 2 hautbois players and 60 privates. In addition the regimental staff consisted of: 1 colonel, 1 lieutenant-colonel, 1 major, 1 quartermaster, 1 adjutant, 1 chaplain, 1 surgeon and a surgeon's mate.

In action the pikemen were 'drawn off' from their companies and formed into a single body, usually deployed between two 'wings' of musketeers. The tactical doctrines employed were undergoing considerable changes during this period. The old method of firing by ranks, which returned to the rear to reload, was being replaced by the Dutch technique of platoon fire. This new method allowed a greater weight of fire to be laid down by a tighter formation, which no longer required spaces between the files, down which the musketeer would retire to reload. Equally, if not more, importantly, the platoons were arranged so that at any one time at least part of the unit was able to give fire, improving the security and fire control of the battalion.

Clothing, Arms and Equipment

Soldiers wore a large collarless coat, usually red, with linings which showed at the cuffs in various colours to difference the units. Small black hats were the norm, edged with white or yellow tape according to whether the buttons were white (pewter) or yellow (brass) metal. Vests or waistcoats were sleeved and usually made up of the soldier's old coat when it was replaced. Small clothes consisted of a linen shirt and cravat in various 'off-white' shades. Breeches were cut less full than earlier in the century and were worn with woollen stockings and heavy black shoes with square toes. Swords were originally carded on buff shoulder belts, but these were gradually being replaced by waist belts. Most pikemen wore no armour, although a few retained back- and breastplates; the wearing of hats, rather than helmets, was universal. The musketeer's collar of charges was, likewise, in decline; the replacement being the cartridge box, usually on a shoulder belt, but sometimes carried on the waist. The matchlock musket was also being replaced by the flintlock and with most regiments fielding them in equal numbers in 1685. The matchlocks had probably disappeared by the end of the century. A more short-term piece of equipment was the plug bayonet (see Plate 14, J and Plate 16) which was only introduced after 1689 into the British Army, but had been replaced just a decade later by the more practical ring bayonet, which allowed the soldier to continue firing when the bayonet was fixed.

The Regiments (1685–1702), Their Commanders and Their Uniforms

The First Regiment of Foot Guards
Formed: 1660
Colonels:
14.12.81 Henry Fitzroy, 1st Duke of Grafton

30.11.88 Sir Edward Henry Lee, 1st Earl of Lichfield
31.12.88 Grafton (reappointed)
16.03.89 Henry, Earl of Romney
27.12.90 Charles, Duke of Schomberg
20.11.93 Romney (reappointed)

Uniform: see Plate 16, A. Grenadier details refer to the period *c*.1685. Officer's grenadier costume (gold lace) is taken from the Francis Hawley portrait. An alternative cap is shown on the right.

The Second (or Coldstream) Regiment of Foot Guards

Formed: 1660
Colonels:
06.01.70 William Craven, 1st Earl Craven
01.05.89 Thomas Tollemache (also spelled Tolmash)
03.10.94 John Lord Cutts

Uniform: see Plate 16, B. Grenadiers' yellow lace.

The Scots Regiment of Foot Guards (on the Scottish establishment)

Formed: 1660
Colonels:
13.06.84 The Hon. James Douglas
01.09.91 The Hon. George Ramsay

Uniform: see Plate 16, C. Grenadiers' coats either white or no lace. Grenadiers probably in fur caps (see 16, F-i).

The Royal Regiment of Foot (Royal Scots)

Formed: 1633
Colonels:
21.10.55 Lord Archibald Douglas, 1st Earl of Dumbarton
31.12.88 Frederick Herman, Duke of Schomberg
05.03.91 Sir Robert Douglas
01.08.92 Lord George Hamilton

Uniform: see Plate 16, D. Grenadiers' white lace edged blue. Grenadiers' cap white fronted with a 'lion face crowned proper'.

The Queen Dowager's Regiment of Foot (the Old Tangier Regiment or Kirke's Lambs)

Formed: 1661
Colonels:
19.04.82 Percy Kirke
18.12.91 William Selwyn

Uniform: see Plate 16, D. Grenadiers in fur caps. Grenadiers' lace green and white (some sources show no lace).

The Holland Regiment (the Buffs)

Formed: 1665
Colonels:
26.01.84 John Sheffield, 3rd Earl Mulgrave

23.10.85 Sir Theophilus Oglethorpe
31.12.88 Charles Churchill
Uniform: see Plate 16, G. Facing colour often described as 'flesh colour'. Coat usually called carmine, i.e. a darker red than most other regiments.

Prince George of Denmark's Regiment of Foot
Served as marines. Known as the Maritime Regiment or the 'Old Marines'.
Formed: 1664. Disbanded: 1690–91
Colonels:
15.02.68 Sir Charles Littleton
Uniform: see Plate 17, C. Red coat worn from 1686. Grey hats worn with yellow coats.

The Queen Consort's Regiment of Foot (The New Tangier Regiment)
Formed: 1680 (later 4th Foot)
Colonels:
23.04.82 Charles Trelawney
01.12.88 Sir Charles Orby
31.12.88 Trelawney (reappointed)
01.01.92 Henry Trelawney
Uniform: See Plate 16, H. Pike armour appears to have been worn as late as 1697. Grenadiers may have worn tall fur caps with a red bag (see Plate 17, K-i).

There were three English and three Scots regiments in Dutch service who came over with William in 1688. They had been in Holland since 1674 and the three Scots regiments returned to the Dutch establishment in 1698. Of the three English regiments, two remained on the English establishment after the Nine Years' War (later becoming the 5th and 6th Regiments of Foot) and one was disbanded in 1698. Although they fit into the list of regiments at this point their dress, organisation and appointments were, at least immediately after 1688, Dutch and will therefore he covered elsewhere.

The Royal Regiment. of Fuzileers
Formed: 1685 (later 7th Foot)
Colonels:
11.06.85 George Legge, 1st Lord Dartmouth
26.08.89 John, Lord Churchill (later 1st Duke of Marlborough)
23.01.93 Lord George Hamilton
01.08.92 Edward Fitzpatrick
12.11.96 Sir Charles O'Hara
Uniform: see Plate 16, L. Cartridge box on a waist belt. Some sources show coats laced white. All rankers and NCOs wore cap. Officers wore gold lace.

Princess Anne of Denmark's Regiment of Foot
Formed: 1685 (later 8th Foot)
Colonels:
19.06.85 Robert Shirley, 1st Earl Fetters
01.11.86 James Fitzjames, 1st Duke of Berwick

31.12.88 John Beaumont
26.12.95 John Richmond Webb
Uniform: See Plate 16, K

Henry Cornwall's Regiment of Foot

Formed: 1685 (later 9th Foot)
Colonels:
19.06.85 Henry Cornwall
20.11.88 Oliver Nicholas
31.12.88 John Cunningham
01.05.89 William Smart
Uniform: see Plate 16, M. Officers are recorded as wearing blue coats with gold lace.

The Earl of Bath's Regiment of Foot

Formed: 1685 (later 10th Foot)
Colonels:
20.06.85 John Granville, 1st Earl of Bath
08.12.88 Sir Charles Carney
31.12.88 Bath (reappointed)
29.10.93 Sir Bevil Granville
Uniform: see Plate 16, J

The Duke of Beaufort's Regiment of Foot

Formed: 1685 (later 11th Foot)
Colonels:
20.06.85 Henry Somerset, 1st Duke of Beaufort
26.10.85 Charles Somerset, Marquess of Worcester
08.05.87 William Herbert, 2nd Marquess of Powis
31.12.88 Sir John Hanmer, Bt.
Uniform: see Plate 16, N. Grenadiers wore tawny and white lace. Caps as 17, K-iii and K-iv with red bags 'turned-up' tawny.

The Duke or Norfolk's Regiment of Foot

Formed: 1685 (later 12th Foot)
Colonels:
20.06.85 Henry Howard, 7th Duke of Norfolk
14.06.86 Sir Edward Henry Lee, Bt., 1st Earl of Lichfield
30.11.88 Sir Robert Carey, 6th Lord Hunsdon
31.12.88 The Hon. Henry Wharton
01.11.89 Richard Brewer
Uniform: see Plate 16, E. Pikemen wore white sashes around their waists.

The Earl of Huntingdon's Regiment of Foot

Formed: 1689 (later 13th Foot)
Colonels:
22.06.85 Theophilus Hastings, 7th Earl of Huntingdon
31.12.88 Ferdinando Hastings

13.03.95 Sir John Jacob
Uniform: See Plate 16, Q. One source shows brass buttons. Grenadiers probably fur caps. See also See Plate 20a for ensign's attire.

Sir Edward Hales' Regiment of Foot
Formed: 1685 (later 14th Foot)
Colonels:
    22.06.85 Sir Edward Hales, Bt.
    31.12.88 William Beveridge (Sapherson dates his appointment to 28.02.89)
    14.11.92 John Tidcomb
Uniform: see Plate 17, A.

Sir William Clifton's Regiment of Foot
Formed: 1685 (later 15th Foot)
Colonels:
    22.06.85 Sir William Clifton, Bt.
    12.05.86 Arthur Herbert, 1st Earl of Torrington
    12.04.87 The Hon. Sackville Tufton
    31.12.88 Sir James Leslie (or Lesley)
    01.11.95 Emmanuel Howe
Uniform: red coat, lined red. White stockings. Grenadier caps (1689) 17, K-iii and K-iv.

John Hales' Regiment of Foot
Formed: 1688. Disbanded: 1698
Colonels:
    10.03.88 John Hales
    26.09.92 Robert Goodwyn
    31.10.93 Edward Dutton Colt
Uniform: red coat, grey stockings, yellow hat lace.

Henry Gage's Regiment of Foot
Formed: 1688. Disbanded 1689.
Colonels:
    27.09.88 Henry Gage
Uniform: not known.

The Duke of Newcastle's Regiment of Foot
Formed: 1688. Disbanded: 1689
Colonels:
    29.09.88 Henry Cavendish, 2nd Duke of Newcastle
Uniform: not known.

Archibald Douglas' Regiment of Foot
Formed: 1688 (later 16th Foot)
Colonels:
    09.10.88 Archibald Douglas
    31.12.88 Robert Hodges

01.08.92 The Hon. James Stanley
Uniform: See Plate 17, B. Coat possibly lined red with a red waistcoat until 1691.

Bevil Skelton's Regiment of Foot
Formed: 1688. Disbanded: 1689
Colonels:
09.10.88 Bevil Skelton
Uniform: not known.

The Earl of Stafford's Regiment of Foot
Formed: 1688. Disbanded: 1689
Colonels:
08.11.88 Henry Stafford-Howard, 10th Earl of Stafford
Uniform: not known.

Edward Fitzpatrick's Regiment of Foot
Formed: 1688. Disbanded: 1698
Colonels:
31.12.88 Edward Fitzpatrick
01.08.92 Francis Collingwood
01.07.99 Edward Fox
Uniform: see Plate 17, D.

Lord Forbes' Regiment of Foot (from 1695 the 'Royal Irish')
Formed: 1684? (later 18th Foot)
Colonels:
01.03.86 Arthur, Lord Forbes
01.03.89 Sir John Edgeworth
01.05.92 Edward, Earl of Meath
19.12.92 Frederick Hamilton
Uniform: see Plate 17, E, worn from 1695, previous facings unknown

Sir David Colyear's Regiment of Foot
Formed: 1688. Disbanded: 1700
Colonel:
31.12.88 Sir David Colyear
Uniform: not known.

The Earl of Monmouth's Regiment of Foot
Formed: 1688. Disbanded: 1698?
Colonels:
10.11.88 Charles, Viscount Mordaunt, Earl of Monmouth
28.04.94 Henry Mordaunt
Uniform: see Plates 17, F and 17, J. Grenadier cap is guesswork, could just as easily have been fur.

Sir John Guise's Regiment of Foot

Formed: 1688. Disbanded: 1695–96
Colonels:
    12.11.88 Sir John Guise
    20.09.89 John Foulkes
    30.11.93 Luke Lillingston
Uniform: not known.

Francis Luttrell's Regiment of Foot

Formed: 1688 (Later 19th Foot)
Colonels:
    20.11.88 Francis Luttrell
    01.01.91 Thomas Erle
Uniform: see Plate 17, N. This regiment was commanded from 1691 by Thomas Erle and may have worn the red faced uniform of his other regiment from that time (see below).

Sir Robert Peyton's Regiment of Foot

Formed: 1688 (Later 20th Foot)
Colonels:
    20.11.88 Sir Robert Peyton
    01.06.89 Gustavus Hamilton
Uniform: coat red, lined red; blue waistcoat, yellow hat lace. Grey stockings.

The Scots Regiment of Fuzileers

Formed: 1678 (later 21st Foot)
Colonels:
    23.09.78 Charles Erskine, 5th Earl of Mar
    29.07.86 Thomas Buchan
    01.03.89 Francis Fergus O'Farrell
    13.01.95 Robert Mackay
    01.01.97 Archibald Row
Uniform: see Plate 17, M. Known as the 'Earl O'Mar's grey breeks', from the colour of their breeches. A source for the period of Marlborough's wars shows yellow stockings.

The Duke of Bolton's 1st Regiment of Foot

Formed: 1689. Disbanded: 1698
Colonels:
    08.03.89 Charles, Marquess of Winchester Duke of Bolton
Uniform: blue coats.

The Duke of Bolton's 2nd Regiment of Foot

Formed: 1689. Disbanded: 1697
Colonels:
    08.03.89 Charles Marquess of Winchester Duke of Bolton
    24.09.92 Godfrey Lloyd
    01.01.95 Henry Holt
Uniform: blue coats.

The Duke of Norfolk's Regiment of Foot
Formed: 1689 (later 22nd Foot)
Colonels:
    08.03.89 Henry, Duke of Norfolk
    28.09.89 Sir Henry Bellasis
Uniform: coats red, lined red (one source shows buff/flesh facings with yellow lace hat and white buttons), grey waistcoat and breeches. White lace and buttons; officers, gold.

Lord Herbert's Regiment of Foot
Formed: 1689 (later 23rd Foot)
Colonels:
    08.03.89 Henry, Lord Herbert of Cherbury
    10.04.89 Charles Herbert
    13.07.91 Toby Purcell
    20.04.92 Sir John Morgan
    28.02.93 Richard lngoldsby
Uniform: coat blue, lined white. White breeches and stockings. White buttons and hat lace.

Sir Edward Dering's Regiment of Foot
Formed: 1689 (later 24th Foot)
Colonels:
    08.03.89 Sir Edward Dering
    27.09.89 Daniel Dering
    01.06.91 Samuel Venner
    13.03.95 Louis, Marquis de Puizar
Uniform: blue coats and breeches.

Lord Lisburne's Regiment of Foot
Formed: 1689. Disbanded: 1698
Colonels:
    08.03.89 Adam. Viscount Lisburne
    01.02.92 Richard Coote
Uniform: coats blue, lined orange or dark buff. Buff or grey breeches. Officers wore crimson coats.

Lord Lovelace's Regiment of Foot
Formed: 1689. Disbanded: 1694
Colonels:
    08.03.89 John, Lord Lovelace
    28.09.89 Nicholas Sankey

The Earl of Drogheda's Regiment of Foot
Formed: 1689. Disbanded: by 1693
Colonels:
    08.03.89 Henry, Earl of Drogheda
Uniform: coats blue, lined white.

The Earl of Kingston's Regiment of Foot
Formed: 1689. Disbanded: 1698
Colonels:
08.03.89 William. Earl of Kingston
??.09.90 The Hon. James Douglas
05.02.92 Henry Rowe
13.03.95 Thomas Brudenell
Uniform: coats red, lined red.

Lord Castleton's Regiment of Foot
Formed: 1689. Disbanded: 1698
Colonels:
08.03.89 George, Viscount Castleton
06.11.94 Thomas Saunderson
Uniform: see Plate 17, L. Breeches red or grey.

Sir Henry lngoldsby's Regiment of Foot
Formed: 1689. Disbanded: 1694
Colonels:
08.03.89 Sir Henry lngoldsby
08.11.89 Richard lngoldsby
Uniform: not known.

Sir Thomas Gower's Regiment of Foot
Formed: 1689. Disbanded: 1698
Colonels:
08.03.89 Sir Thomas Gower
28.10.89 Henry, Earl of Drogheda
Uniform: not known.

Thomas Erle's Regiment of Foot
Formed: 1689. Disbanded: 1698
Colonels:
08.03.89 Thomas Erle
Uniform: red, lined yellow.

The Earl of Roscommon's Regiment of Foot
Formed: 1689. Disbanded: by 1692
Colonels:
08.03.89 Cary, Earl of Roscommon
Uniform: red coats.

Isaac de la Meloniere's Regiment of Foot (French Huguenot regiment)
Formed: 1689. Disbanded:1697
Colonels:
01.04.89 Major-General Isaac de la Meloniere
Uniform: probably grey coats.

Francis de Cambon's Regiment of Foot (French Huguenot)
Formed: 1689 Disbanded: 1697
Colonels:
    11.04.89 Francis de Cambon
    12.08 93 William, Count de Matron
Uniform: probably grey coats.

The Marquis de Caillemotte's Regiment of Foot
Formed: 1689. Disbanded: 1697
Colonels:
    01.04.89 Marquis de Caillemotte
    19.07.90 Peter de Belcastel
Uniform: probably grey coats.

Gustavus Hamilton's (Inniskilling) Regiment of Foot
Formed: 1689. Disbanded: 1698
Colonels:
    20.06.89 Gustavus Hamilton
    13.07.91 Abraham Creighton
Uniform: red coats lined red. Red or blue breeches. Red stockings. Officers wore blue coats.

Thomas Lloyd's (Inniskilling) Regiment of Foot
Formed: 1689. Disbanded: by 1694
Colonels:
    20.06.89 Thomas Lloyd
    01.03.90 Lord George Hamilton
Uniform: not known.

Henry Baker's (Londonderry) Regiment of Foot
Formed: 1689. Disbanded: 1698
Colonels:
    1689 Henry Baker (Governor of Londonderry)
    04.08.89 Thomas St. John
Uniform: not known.

The Rev. George Walker's (Londonderry) Regiment of Foot
Formed: 1689. Disbanded: 1691
Colonels:
    19.04.89 – George Walker
    04.08.89 –Robert White
    October 89 – John Caulfield
Uniform: not known.

The Earl of Leven's Regiment of Foot
Formed: 1689 (later 25th Foot)
Colonels:
    19.03.89 David, Earl of Leven

19.03.94 James Maitland
Uniform: probably red coats, lined white. Grey breeches.

The Earl of Angus's Regiment of Foot
Formed: 1689 (later 26th Foot)
Colonels:
    19.03.89 James, Earl of Angus
    01.08.92 Andrew Monto
    25.08.93 James Ferguson
Uniform: carmine[1] coats, lined white. White waistcoat and breeches. Yellow hat lace and buttons (an alternative source shows yellow cuffs and breeches and blue bonnets).

Zachariah Tiffin's Regiment of Foot
Formed: 1689 (later 27th Foot)
Colonels:
    20.06.89 Zachariah Tiffin
Uniform: coats light grey, lined white or yellow (off-white?), grey breeches and stockings.

The Earl of Argyll's Regiment of Foot
Formed: 1689. Disbanded: 1698
Colonels:
    19.04.89 Archibald. Earl of Argyll
    07.04.94 John, Lord Lorne
Uniform: not known.

Lord Bargeney's Regiment of Foot
Formed: 1689. Disbanded: 1689
Colonel:
    19.04.89 John, Lord Bargeney
Uniform: not known.

Lord Blantyre's Regiment of Foot
Formed: 1689. Disbanded: 1689
Colonel:
    19.04.89 John, Lord Blantyre
Uniform: not known.

The Laird of Grant's Regiment of Foot
Formed: 1689. Disbanded: 1690
Colonel:
    19.04.89 Ludovic Grant
Uniform: not known.

---

1   A purplish-red pigment, made from dye obtained from the cochineal beetle; carminic acid or any of its derivatives.

The Earl of Glencairn's Regiment of Foot
Formed: 1689. Disbanded: 1691
Colonel:
    19.04.89 John, Earl of Glencairn
Uniform: not known

Lord Kenmuir's Regiment of Foot
Formed: 1689. Disbanded: 1691
Colonel:
    19.04.89 Alexander, Viscount Kenmuir
Uniform: probably red coats, lined white. May have served at Killiekrankie in 'hodden[2] grey' with blue bonnets.

The Earl of Mar's Regiment of Foot
Formed: 1689. Disbanded: 1689
Colonel:
    19.04.89 Charles, Earl of Mar
Uniform: not known.

Lord Strathnaver's Regiment of Foot (I)
Formed: 1689. Disbanded 1690
Colonel:
    19.04.89 John, Lord Strathnaver
Uniform: not known.

Richard Cunningham's Regiment of Foot
Formed: 1689. Disbanded: 1698
Colonels:
    18.12.89 Richard Cunningham
    01.02.91 John Buchan
Uniform: not known.

The 1st Marine Regiment
Formed: 1690. Disbanded: 1698
Colonels:
    16.01.90 Arthur, Earl of Torrington
    31.12.90 Peregrine, Earl of Derby
Uniform: see Plate 17, Q. All grenadiers' caps and flintlocks.

The 2nd Marine Regiment
Formed: 1690. Disbanded: 1698
Colonels:
    17.01.90 Thomas, Earl of Pembroke and Montgomery
    01.01.91 Henry Killigrew
    01.12.93 John, Lord Berkeley

---

2   A coarse cloth made of undyed wool.

01.03.97 Sir Cloudesley Shovell
Uniform: see above.

John Hill's Regiment of Foot
Formed: 1690. Disbanded: 1698
Colonel:
    02.09.90 John Hill
Uniform: not known.

The Earl of Donegal's Regiment of Foot
Formed: 1693. Disbanded: 1698
Colonel:
    01.02.93 Arthur, Earl of Donegal
Uniform: not known.

Sir James Moncrieff's Regiment of Foot
Formed: 1693. Disbanded: 1714
Colonels:
    01.02.93 Sir James Moncrieff
    01.01.94 George Hamilton
Uniform: not known.

Lord Strathnaver's Regiment of Foot (II)
Formed: 1693. Disbanded: 1717
Colonels:
    01.02.93 John, Lord Strathnaver
Uniform: not known.

Robert Mackay's Regiment of Foot
Formed: 1694. Disbanded: 1697
Colonels:
    01.01.94 Robert Mackay
    13.11.95 George McGill
Uniform: not known.

Sir John Gibson's Regiment of Foot
Formed: 1694. Disbanded: 1698
Colonel:
    16.02.94 Sir John Gibson
Uniform: not known.

Thomas Farrington's Regiment of Foot
Formed: 1694. Disbanded: 1698
Colonel:
    16.02.94 Thomas Farrington
Uniform: not known.

Francis Russell's Regiment of Foot
Formed: 1694. Disbanded: 1697
Colonel:
    16.02.94 Francis Russell
Uniform: not known.

Lord John Murray's Regiment of Foot
Formed: 1694. Disbanded: 1697
Colonels:
    23.03.94 Lord John Murray
Uniform: not known.

Lord John Lindsay's Regiment of Foot
Formed: 1694. Disbanded: 1697
Colonel:
    23.04.94 John, Lord Lindsay
Uniform: white coats, lined red. White breeches, red stockings. Sergeants: grey coats, red breeches and stockings.

John Courthorpe's Regiment of Foot
Formed: 1694. Disbanded: 1698
Colonel:
    23,04.94 John Courthorpe
Uniform: not known.

Sir Richard Atkins's Regiment of Foot
Formed: 1694. Disbanded: 1698
Colonels:
    23,04.94 Sir Richard Atkins
    06.12.96 George Villiers
Uniform: not known.

Viscount Mountjoy's Regiment of Foot
Formed: 1694. Disbanded: 1698
Colonel:
    23.04.94 William, Viscount Mountjoy
Uniform: not known.

Viscount Charlemont's Regiment of Foot
Formed: 1694. Disbanded 1698
Colonel:
    23.04.94 William, Viscount Charlemont
Uniform: not known.

Luke Lillingston's Regiment of Foot
Formed: 1694. Disbanded: 1698
Colonel:
    24.12.94 Luke Lillingston

Uniform: not known.

Sir William Douglas' Regiment of Foot
Formed: 1695. Disbanded: 1697
Colonel:
    1695 William Douglas
Uniform: not known.

The 3rd Marine Regiment
Formed: 1698. Disbanded; 1698
Colonel:
    19.08.98 Thomas Brundell
Uniform: not known.

The 4th Marine Regiment
Formed: 1698. Disbanded: 1698
Colonel:
    19.08.98 William Seymour
Uniform: not known.

The 5th Marine Regiment
Formed: 1698. Disbanded: 1698
Colonel:
    19.08.98 Edward Dutton Colt
Uniform: not known.

The 6th Marine Regiment
Colonel:
    19.08.98 Henry Mordaunt
Uniform: not known.

Part Three: Colours

As in the period of the Civil War all companies of a regiment were issued with a company colour, the exception to this rule being the grenadier company which, owing to the nature of its work, did not carry a flag. The organisation of the grenadier company reflected this by fielding an extra lieutenant in place of the company ensign. Colours of this period are still of the large dimensions used during the 1640s, being approximately six feet square with the staff still short enough to allow the colours to be carried and displayed 'properly' according to the vales of seventeenth century etiquette, unlike later when smaller colours were carded on longer poles.

The Foot Guard
Traditionally the regiments of Guards had had their captains' colours differenced by the use of badges depicting heraldic beasts and symbols used at various times by the monarchs of England, but on his succession King

James II introduced a simpler system as follows:

1st Regiment of Foot Guards
- Standard of his Majesty's Company: crimson embroidered in the centre with the Royal crown and cypher (i.e. JR) (see Plate 18, A1)
- Colonel's Company: plain crimson
- Lieutenant-Colonel's Company: white with crimson cross of St. George throughout, in the centre of cross an imperial crown in gold.
- Major's Company: as lieutenant-colonel with a crimson pile wavy (see Plate 18, A2)
- 1st Captain's Company: white with crimson cross of St. George throughout in the centre of the cross the Royal crown and cypher.
- 2nd to 20th Captains' Companies: as the 1st Captain's colour with the relevant number of cyphers on the field of the cross.

In 1689 the cyphers were changed to those of William and Mary and the colonel's colour, plain under King James, was now decorated with golden crowns in the comers, but remained crimson (see Plate 18, B3 and B4). King William also reintroduced the company badges in use during Charles ll's reign. These badges were as follows:

- I Captain: The Royal crest of a crown surmounted by a lion
- II Captain: A crowned golden rose (all remaining badges are also crowned)
- III Captain: A golden fleur-de-Lys
- IV Captain: A golden portcullis
- V Captain: A white rose surrounded by the rays of a golden sun
- VI Captain: A golden thistle, the stalk and leaves proper
- VII Captain: A golden harp
- VIII Captain: A golden dragon
- IX Captain: A white greyhound with golden collar and chains
- X Captain: A golden sun
- XI Captain: A white unicorn with golden horn, mane and hooves
- XII Captain: A white antelope with golden horns, coronet and chains
- XIII Captain: A white hart with golden horns, coronet and chains
- XIV Captain: A white falcon within a golden fetterlock
- XV Captain: A golden rose, with stalk and leaves of the same
- XVI Captain: A white swan with a golden coronet and chain
- XVII Captain: A falcon crowned and carrying a golden sceptre in his raised talon
- XVIII Captain: A golden tree stump with leaves of the same
- XIX Captain: crossed sword and sceptre in gold
- XX Captain: The Royal Oak in gold

The seniority of the captains was further emphasised by the painting of Roman numerals in black, in the top canton nearest the staff. Likewise in 1685 the 2nd Foot Guards carried the following colours:

2nd or Coldstream Regiment of Foot Guards
- Colonel's Company: plain white
- Lieutenant-Colonel's Company: white with a crimson cross of St. George throughout
- Major's Company: As lieutenant-colonel's with the addition of a crimson pile wavy (see Plate 18, A3)
- 1st to 9th Captains' Companies: as lieutenant-colonel's with the addition of Roman numerals in gold crowned with an imperial crown (see Plate 18, A4).

William III altered the flags only slightly by adding the crowned Royal Cypher in gold to the centre of the cross on the lieutenant-colonel's and major's colours.

The following colours of the Scots Guards, dating from the reign of James III, are known:

Scots Guards
- Colonel's Company: plain white
- Lieutenant-Colonel's Company: blue field with a white cross of St. Andrew.
- Major's Company: As lieutenant-colonel's with the addition of a red pile wavy (see Plate 18, B1)
- 1st Captain's Company: as lieutenant-colonel's with a Roman numeral in white on the blue above the cross (see Plate 18, B2).

It seems reasonable to assume that the other captains' colours carried the correct numerals in the same place. No details exist of specific changes to the colours of the Scots Guards made by William III, however a colour captured at Dixmunde attributed to the regiment (see Plate 18, C2) has a colour identical to that of the lieutenant-colonel's under King James which was lost at Neerwinden.

The regiments of the line carried the following identified colours:

The Royal Regiment of Foot (Royal Scots)
Under James II:
- Colonel's Company: white with centre device as per Plate 18, C3.
- Lieutenant-Colonel's Company: blue field, white cross of St. Andrew centre, device as per Plate 18, C3.
- Major's Company: see Plate 18, C3.
- 1st to 20th Captains' Companies: as lieutenant-colonel's with addition of silver/white Roman numeral on blue field above cross (see Plate 18, C4).
- Under William III: see Plate 18, D3 and D4, colours captured at Neerwinden and attributed to the Royal Scots.

The Queen Dowager's Regiment of Foot (the Old Tangier Regiment or

Kirke's Lambs)

Under James II:

- Colonel's Company: plain green, centre device as per Plate 18, D1.
- Lieutenant-colonel's Company: as 18, D1 without the numeral.
- Major's Company: as lieutenant-colonel's with the addition of a gold pile wavy.
- 1st to 9th Captains' Companies: see 18, D1 with correct changes of numeral. Some sources show the numerals positioned in the upper canton next to the staff rather than on the cross.
- Under William III: no confirmed evidence. 18, D3 has been attributed, but this seems very unlikely. Probably carried a version of 18, D1 either without the cypher or with one applicable to the new monarchs.

The Holland Regiment (The Buffs)

Under James II:

- Colonel's Company: plain black, centre device as per 18, E1.
- Lieutenant-Colonel's Company: as 18, E1 without the numeral.
- Major's Company: as 18, E1, but with a gold pile wavy replacing the numeral
- 1st to 9th Captains': as 18, E1 with correct numerals.
- Without the saltire. Colonel's colour may possibly have been plain
- 1685, Colonel's Company: as 19, K3 yellow.

Under William III:

- Captured at Neerwinden in 1683, see Plate 18, E2 and another colour.
- Under James II:

Prince George of Denmark's Regiment of Foot (served as Marines, known as the Maritime Regiment or the 'Old Marines')

Under James II:

- Colonel's Company: plain yellow (see Plate 18, E3).
- Lieutenant-Colonel's Company: yellow, red cross of St. George edged white.
- Major's and all Captains' Companies: as 18, E4.

Under William III:

- Probably the same, regiment disbanded in 1690–91.

The Queen Consort's Regiment of Foot (the New Tangier Regiment)

Under James II:

- Pre-1686: yellow field with red cross of St. George and sun rays device (see Plate 19, F1). Post-1686:
- Colonel's Company: plain white, centre device of the Queen Consort's cypher.
- Lieutenant-Colonel's Company: as 19, F2 minus the pile wavy.
- Major's Company: as 19, F2
- All Captains' Companies: as lieutenant-colonel's with the addition of the Queen consort's cypher.

Under William III:

- No details, probably a variation on 19, F1.

The Royal Regiment of Fuzileers
Under James II:
- Colonel's Company: as 19, G3.
- Lieutenant-Colonel's Company: as 19, G4 minus the central device.
- Major's Company: as lieutenant-colonel's with the addition of a red pile wavy.
- All Captains' Companies: as 19, G4

Under William III: Probably the same.

Princess Anne of Denmark's Regiment of Foot

Under James II:
- 1685: Colonel's Company: as 18, D3
- Lieutenant-Colonel's Company: as 19, K4 minus the pile wavy,
- Major's: as 19, K4
- 1st to 9th Captains' Companies: the Princess' cypher depicted on the cross, the number of cyphers differencing the companies.
- 1687: 1st to 9th Captains' Companies: Princess' cypher in centre of cross, with white Roman numerals in upper staff side canton.

Under William III:
- Probably the same.

Henry Cornwall's Regiment of Foot
Under James II:
- Colonel's Company: plain orange.
- Lieutenant-Colonel's Company: as 19, F3 minus the pile wavy
- Major's Company: as 19, F3
- 1st to 9th Captains' Companies: as lieutenant-colonel's, differenced by white roundels (see Plate 19, F4 for 3rd Captain's colour).

Under William III:
- Possibly the same.

The Earl of Bath's Regiment of Foot
Under James II:
- Colonel's Company: plain yellow.
- Lieutenant-Colonel's Company: as 18, D3 minus centre device.
- Major's Company: as lieutenant-colonel's with the addition of a red pile wavy.
- All Captains' Companies: as 18, D1. No form of differencing is apparent.

Under William III:
- Probably the same.

The Duke of Beaufort's Regiment of Foot
Under James II:
- Colonel's Company: plain crimson.
- Lieutenant-Colonel's Company: as 18, D2 minus centre device.
- Major's Company: as lieutenant-colonel's with the addition of a white

pile wavy.
- All Captains' Companies: as 18, D2, no form of differencing is apparent.

Under William III:
- Possibly the same.

The Duke of Norfolk's Regiment of Foot
Under James II:
- Colonel's Company: As 19, H1.
- Lieutenant-colonel's Company: as 19, H2 minus centre device.
- Major's Company: as lieutenant-colonel's with the addition of a white pile wavy.
- All Captains' Companies: as 19, H2, no form of differencing is apparent. In 1686 the Duke resigned his commission and it is recorded that the field of the colours was changed to white, no details of the devices used on the new colours is known.

Under William III:
- Nothing known. These colours, or something similar, may have been carried by the Duke of Norfolk's regiment of 1689 (later Sir Henry Bellasis).

The Earl of Huntingdon's Regiment of Foot
Under James II:
- Probably variations on the yellow field, red cross of St. George etc. (see 19, J1 and J2, as Hastings).

Sir Edward Hales' Regiment of Foot
Under James II:
- Colonel's Company: plain red
- Lieutenant-Colonel's Company: as H3 minus centre device.
- Major's: as lieutenant-colonel's with the addition of a white pile wavy.
- 1st to 9th Captains' Companies: differenced by the use of the correct number of roundels on the body of the cross (see Plate 19, H3 for 3rd Captain's colour).

Under William III:
- Probably the same.

Sir William Clifton's Regiment of Foot
Under James II:
- Colonel's Company: as 19, J3.
- Lieutenant-Colonel's Company: as J4 minus centre device.
- Major's Company: as lieutenant-colonel's with the addition of a white pile wavy.
- All Captains' Companies: as 19, J4 with no differencing apparent.

Under William III:
- Not known.

Archibald Douglas' Regiment of Foot
Under James II:

- Ede-Borrett quotes 'one modern source' as giving the colours as 'a white field with all except the Colonel's, having the cross of St. George overall'.

Under William III:

- Not known.

Lord Forbes' Regiment of Foot (from 1695 the 'Royal Irish')

Condray shows a colour appearing to date from Marlborough's wars but possibly carried earlier, it has a red St. Patrick's cross on a white field. There is a golden harp crowned with an imperial crown surmounted by a lion with overall a ribbon carrying a motto which appears to be: 'NAMURCENSIS PROEMPTEM'.

Sir David Colyear's Regiment of Foot

Probably arrangements of St. Andrew's cross, thistles etc.

The Scots Regiment of Fuzileers

Under James II:

- Colonel's Company: white centre device as per 19, K1.
- Lieutenant-Colonel's Company: as 19, K1
- Major's Company: as 18, C2
- 1st to 9th Captains' Companies: as 19, K1 with seniority denoted by Roman numerals in top left corner.

Under William III:

- Probably the same.
- Finally, in the field William sought to reduce the number of colours carried to three, though this was resisted by the companies. During Queen Anne's reign the numbers were further reduced to two. When the battalion was in combat all colours were carried in the ranks of the regiment's pikemen.

Part Four: Officers' Clothing

Part one covered the dress of the rank and file in the 'marching' regiments of these two 'illustrious' monarchs. Officers' dress was also commented on, but only if there was some considerable difference between that worn by the officer and the uniforms of his men. Examples of this might include Henry Cornwall's or Gustavus Hamilton's Regiments where the men wore red coats and the officers blue; or Lord Lisburne's Regiment where the reverse was the case. It is also certainly the case that regiments such as Lord Kenmuir's, who may have served at Killiekrankie in their everyday 'hodden grey' clothing, would have fielded officers, if not in regimentals, in something approaching the concept of 'gentleman's attire', not in 'hodden grey'! The critical point regarding the uniforms worn by those holding the King's commission is that it was not to be perceived by their peers as uniform. The whole idea of wearing a coat of uniform cut and style, faced with the regimental colours smacked of livery to the gentleman of the late seventeenth century, and livery was worn by footmen and other servants, not by personages such as themselves. Officers would therefore wear a coat in a shade of red different to that of their men, turned up with a colour similar to that of the body of the coat, or perhaps a neutral colour that could not be mistaken for facings. A quick perusal of officers' portraits during the period in question shows a generally sober and conservative approach to clothes and, even in civilian life, gaudy cuffs and decoration were the exception rather than the norm. This contrasts with much of what was being worn in France at the time with a much greater emphasis on the colour of the cloth, the contrast of the cuffs, the latter often with decorative embroidery, and the ribbons.

Note: Stuart Reid, in his excellent book on Killiekrankie, discusses the possibility of Scottish officers wearing something approaching regimental uniform. His point is that as Scots infantry, for the most part, wore uniforms 'turned up' with plain white material, this would not be thought of as the colonel's livery and could be worn without fear. Another consideration is the relative affluence of the English officer class in comparison with those in Scotland, the argument being in favour of expectance of a more uniform dress for financial reasons.

However, two points mitigate against this theory: firstly Childs has shown that huge numbers of Scots took commissions in English regiments, where they presumably refused to wear regimentals, along with their English brother officers. Secondly if any group was to need to resort to this method of avoiding the outlay on clothing it was this group of Scottish officers in English regiments, as any Scot with influence or financial 'clout' was able to purchase a commission on the Scottish establishment.

Some additional information gleaned from Lawson includes:

Francis Cornwall's Regiment
1692: officers, blue coats lined blue with gold loops, gold hat lace; caps, pouches, cartouche boxes of crimson velvet embroidered with gold and silver for the captains and 2 lieutenants of grenadiers.

Sir William Cliffton's Regiment
1690: officers' coat scarlet lined red 'a red coat with plate buttons made up (as a pattern) 3 bearskins for the colonel and 2 Captains' (? for housings).

The next regiment listed by Lawson poses some difficulties. It is described as Lord George Hamilton's Inniskilling Regiment, however he goes on to list Colonel Abraham Creighton as the commander from 1692. Whilst Creighton was a colonel of foot from 1691–98, he had taken over the Inniskilling Regiment of Gustavus Hamilton, not that of George. However Lawson also states that the regiment was raised in 1689 and disbanded in 1692. This is closer to the history of Lord George's regiment which had certainly been disbanded at the latest 1694 and had been previously led by Thomas Lloyd. So I have reorganised these so that the references to 1690 apply to Lord George Hamilton's Regiment (ex-Lloyd's) and those for 1692 apply to Abraham Creighton's Regiment (ex-Gustavus Hamilton's), both these regiments having been raised in Inniskilling on 20 June 1689. As Lord George took up his post in March 1690 and Gustavus only left his regiment in July 1690 for about 16 months, two of the three lnniskilling regiments were commanded by unrelated men called Hamilton! To confuse matters further, following this entry, Lawson then describes the regiment raised by Sir Robert Peyton and taken over by Gustavus Hamilton three weeks before be raised his Inniskilling regiment. Hamilton commanded Peyton's old regiment until April 1706 becoming a major-general and receiving the title Viscount Boyne. Whilst Gustavus was of mixed Irish and Swedish descent, Lord George Hamilton (1666–1737) was a Scot, being the fifth son of the Duke of Hamilton. He served in Ireland from 1689 to 1691 and commanded the Royal Fusiliers, from 1693, at Steenkirk and Namur (where he was wounded). In 1695 he was created the Earl of Orkney, serving Marlborough loyally as a lieutenant-general and later general (1711). He was promoted field marshal the year before his death.Finally it might be useful to list a few more Hamiltons who might cross the path of those studying late-seventeenth century history:

Sir George Hamilton (d. 1676)
Irish Catholic mercenary in French service killed at the battle of Severne in 1676. Had previously served the exiled Charles II.

Richard Hamilton (d. 1717)
Irish Catholic. Fifth son of the above. Possibly the best of the Jacobite generals. In French service until 1685. Commanded regiments of dragoons and horse in King James' army. Major general in November 1688. Deserted King William for King James, having been sent to convince Tyrconnell to side with the Williamites. Fought for Jacobites in Ireland inflicting defeats on the Northern Protestants at Dromore and at the 'Fords' before Derry. Took over the siege of Derry after the two French engineers (Maumont and Pusignan) supplied by Louis XIV were killed in a sortie by the garrison. Fought heroically at the Boyne commanding the horse at OIdbridge after King James' and Lauzun had moved to cover Rosnaree. Led charges to allow the rest of the army to retreat but was wounded and captured. Exchanged in 1692 and joined the Irish Brigade in France. When the possibility of an invasion of the British Isles was removed after the naval Battle of La Hogue, he retired from the army, dying in poverty in Paris in 1717.

Anthony Hamilton (d. 1720)
Younger brother of Richard. Jacobite dragoon colonel (later general) in Ireland, had his command scattered by the lnniskilling forces in an ambush at Lisnaskea. Served at the Boyne. Became a gentleman of letters, dying at the Old Pretender's court at St. Germain in 1720.

John Hamilton (d. 1691)
Youngest of the Hamilton brothers. A colonel of foot and an ally of Tyrconnell against the intrigues of Patrick Sarsfield (who believed him to be a traitor). A major-general in 1691 he served at Athlone, where his covering force failed to repel Ginckel's final attack, and at Aughrim where he was mortally wounded and captured.

Claud Hamilton, Earl of Abercorn
Irish Catholic. Supporter of King James, raising a regiment of horse for his service. After the Jacobite defeat his estates were forfeited and claimed by his brother Charles (who became a Protestant and later 6th Earl).

George Hamilton (d. 1715)
Scottish. Served in the Anglo-Dutch brigade returning to King James' army in 1688. In Williamite service, promoted to colonel, taking command of Sir James Moncrieff's Regiment. A brigadier in Dutch service by 1704, be was badly wounded at Malplaquet. In 1714 he joined the Jacobite rebels in Scotland and was captured, tried and executed.

Thomas Hamilton
Served in the Anglo-Dutch Brigade. Commanded the grenadiers of the Scots Foot Guards and by 1691 was lieutenant-colonel. In Flanders 1691–94. Brevet colonel 1704. Had retired by 1710.

[Author's note: On completing this section of the text and having checked as much as I could find on the 'Hamilton' with my sources I found the following in Kings in Conflict. *The Revolutionary War in Ireland and its Aftermath*, edited by W.A. Maguire, says: 'Another Hamilton, Gustavus (not to be confused with the Gustavus Hamilton who was governor of Enniskillen), who had led the storming of Athlone, got 3.482 Irish acres; he fought under Marlborough and later became the first Viscount Boyne.' Since reading this I have checked nearly 20 different books which refer to Gustavus Hamilton in the text and none mentions either in text or in index that there were two men of the same name serving the Williamite cause and most refer to the Inniskilling colonel as being created Viscount Boyne! I am not sure what to conclude. If anyone reading this has any further information please let me know, via the publisher. Finally, despite his entreaties not to confuse the two Hamiltons, Maguire's own index manages to do so!]

Lord George Hamilton's Regiment (ex–Lloyd's)
1690: 'For Lieutenant-Colonel Hodson's coat, fraize (frieze) 15 yards gold and silk twist, 6 dozen buttons, gold thread'. Captains' coats, scarlet with silver loops, hats laced silver, silver buttons, pair of gloves, pike, powder pouch. Lieutenants' scarlet coats with silver loops and hat lace. Pikes.

Abraham Creighton's Regiment (ex-Gustavus Hamilton's)
1692: officers' coats scarlet lined scarlet shalloon, 120 oiled skins for waistcoats; gold and silver buttons, gold and silver lace fringe, beaver hats and castor hats, gold and silver loops lace, and hat bands, crimson breeches.

Gustavus Hamilton's Regiment (ex-Sir Robert Peyton's, later 20th Foot)
1691: officers' hats with gold edging and bands, silver for subaltern officers, scarlet coats lined scarlet and laced with gold for superior officers and silver for subalterns, buttons to match, grey worsted stockings. Blue surtout coats lined blue. 1692: coats and surtouts as before, gloves laced gold and silver, six horses for the colonel's own use.

Sir Henry Belalyse's Regiment (later 22nd Foot)
1692: Officers' crimson coats lined crimson, gold lace and gold fringe. Silver and gold laced hats; grey waistcoats and breeches.

Lord Cutts' Regiment
1691: Officers' coats crimson lined crimson, faced buff, white stockings (the facing colour was also described as do ve grey, or as Lawson puts it 'a warm yellowish grey colour called Isabelle'. The specific mention of facings as well as lining implies that Cutts' officers wore the regimental facing colour on their coats). See Plate 20a.

Henry Rowe's Regiment (ex-Lord Kingston's)
1692: officers', surgeon's and quartermaster's, coats crimson lined crimson, laced gold and silver, hats laced gold and silver, white worsted stockings.

John Michelburne's Regiment
1691: 40 officers' laced coats, 40 officers' surtout coats, striped calico waistcoats with silver and gold buttons, crimson stockings, white stockings, laced hats. Three beaver hats for the Field Officers … 30 gorgets gilt with gold and silver, orange net sashes, gold and silver laced gloves… 1 scarlet cloak, 4 sets of new housings and holster caps.

Richard Coote's Regiment (ex-Lord Lisburne's)
1692: officers' coats crimson lined crimson and laced with silver, 13 sets of silver loops and buttons for captains, 26 sets for the subalterns.

Gorget and Scarf
The only two official items of dress that were worn by officers of foot were the gorget and scarf. The gorget was the remains of the corselet or back- and breast-plate that had previously been worn, indeed in the official language of the royal warrant of 1684, the gorget is still referred to as a corselet:

> For the better distinction of Our several Officers serving in our companies of Foot and Troops of Dragoons, Our will and Pleasure is that all Captains of Foot and Dragoons wear no other corslet than of gold. All Lieutenants black corslets studded with gold, and the Ensigns corslets of silver...

The gorget at the time of the Civil War had still provided an element of protection even when worn without the rest of the back- and breast-plate, however by the 1680s its size had diminished (see Plate 20, figures H and L) to the point where its use was purely decorative. It was normally held in place by ribbons secured to the holes in the top leading edges and tied behind the neck of the wearer. In the eighteenth century the ribbons were often in the facing colour and this may have been the case earlier.

Whether or not the warrant of 1684 was meant to apply to the Foot Guards regiments, in 1685 in the First and Second Foot Guards: 'The Captains had gorgets of silver plate double gilt, the Lieutenants ones of steel polished and sanguined and studded with nails of gold, and the Ensigns ones of silver plate.' These rank distinctions may have died out as early as 1702, and during the eighteenth century gorgets were ordered first to match the officers' lace colour (gold or silver) and then in 1796 that they should all be gilt.

Scarves were, for the most part, made of silk net and coloured crimson or some other tone of deep red. They were often decorated with lace fringes and it is most likely these fringes that are referred to in the individual regimental cases listed above. There are cases of different colour sashes but these were usually worn by pikemen and rarely by officers. The case of Michelburne's Regiment, listed above, being one exception.

Plate Commentary

Plate 20
A. Perhaps the most famous portrait of an officer, not of held rank, in the history of the early British army. Hawley was captain of the Grenadier Company of the 1st Foot Guards at the beginning of King James' reign transferring to John Berkeley's Dragoons in July 1685. Three years later he was lieutenant-colonel and was killed at Steenkirk in 1692. His cap is turned up with medium blue-green velvet and laced with gold, the bag at the rear being likewise blue-green and the base gold. He is shown with his own hair grown to mid length, without a periwig, and his delicate lawn cravat is decorated in gold. His coat is made of deep red velvet with the buttonholes trimmed in gold. Both the cuffs and the belting are the same blue-green velvet as the cap decorated with gold lace.
B. Portrait of a naval flag officer showing the very simple undecorated styles worn by Englishmen at the turn of the seventeenth century. Apart from gold buttons and buttonhole decorations the whole coat is plain red velvet with a corslet (probably a studio prop) worn over it.
C. This officer wears a fine wool coat of a bright scarlet hue, decorated with silver laced buttonholes and cuff loops. His small tricorn is also laced silver.
D. A field officer posing by an artillery battery in one of Jan Wyck's many views of the Battle of the Boyne. His black hat is laced gold, beneath which he wears a dark colour wig. His medium-grey coat has just a small amount of gold on the cuffs, together with gold buttons which also decorate the waistcoat which is also grey. His breeches are dark red and his boots black. The colour of the saddle housing is not clear, but appears to be dark brown decorated in gold.
E. English colonel from a black and white illustration in a sale catalogue. The coat is probably scarlet similar to **C** with gold or silver lace decoration. The waistcoat is surprisingly silk and very heavily decorated (maybe an off-duty moment).
F. Red coat with a silver shoulder-knot. Dark wig.
G. Mitre cap from a black and white illustration from the National Army Museum's exhibition on the early British army. Colours unknown, but field appears to be dark.
H. Outline of typical subaltern or captain serving on foot. Pike shaft natural wood with a steel head.

J. A portrait of William III attributed to van Wyck and shows how even senior officers' clothing was often quite plain and simply adorned. The hat is dark grey with white feathers and the coat browny-grey edged with gold lace. The waistcoat, as well as the horse furniture, is navy blue decorated more heavily in gold than the coat.

K. Another portrait of the King at the Battle of the Boyne. This time the coat is of bright blue velvet decorated only with gold buttons. However both the waistcoat and housing
are heavily decorated gold on gold.

L. A gorget of the period (see above), the arms shown probably relate, more precisely, to the period following the death of Queen Mary 1694–1702.

4

The French Army in the War of the Grand Alliance

Part One: The Maison du Roi. Infantry of the *Gardes Françaises* and the *Gardes Suisse*

GARDES FRANÇAISES (French Foot Guards)

The regiment dated back to the 1560s with the founding of a regiment of guards for the defence and protection of King Francois II. These were the days of the French Civil or Religious Wars and the life of the monarch was in serious danger, witness the end of Francois' younger brother Henry III who was assassinated in 1589. The regiment went through various changes during this period and it was not until the reign of Henry III's successor, Henry IV, that guards were put on a more regular footing.

Organisation

By the time Louis XIV was on the throne the *Gardes Françaises* had become a brigade. Varying in size between four and six battalions during the 60s, 70s and 80s it was restored to six battalions in 1689 and remained at this strength during the period in question.

Like the French line infantry covered in previous articles the guards were equipped with pikes and matchlock muskets during the War of the Grand Alliance, but unlike other French infantry they were somewhat tardy in raising grenadier companies – not until 1689 (the *Gardes Suisse* didn't have grenadiers until 1691!)

Dress

Until 1661 the guards, like most soldiers of their time, were not uniformed, wearing civilian style with certain military characteristics. The first uniform was grey with red linings and cuffs, whilst officers wore red. The sergeants of the regiment were the first to adopt blue, in the 1670s, with the guards taking up their famous blue and red in 1685. At first the uniform was unlaced, but soon the famous white lace began to be placed on the front edge and pockets and later on the cuffs. Throughout the period the breeches and stockings were red.

Marechal de Camp
1. Francois d'Aubusson, Duc de la Feuillade
2. 1691 Louis Francois, Marquis (later Duc) de Boufflers
3. 1704 Antoine de Grammont, Duc de Guiche

Service Record

In 1689 the six battalions of the *Gardes Françaises* were sent to Flanders to join the army of Marechal d'Humieres. The regiment took part in the French defeat at the battle of Walcourt where it came under heavy fire while assaulting the town. Susane (*Histoire l'Infanterie Francaise*) gives the officer casualties as four captains, two lieutenants and 21 others. The guards spent the rest of the campaign in the marching and countermarching which was such a part of the warfare of the late seventeenth century. On 3 October the regiment left Flanders to join the forces on the Rhine under the Marechal de Lorges. During this time Captain Maulmont of the Guards, serving in the Jacobite army of James II, was killed at the siege of Londonderry. The following year four guards battalions were at Fleurus, where they served on the extreme right of the French line (the senior regiment of an army was always accorded the right to take this 'place of honour'). All six battalions were present when the King commanded in person at the siege of Mons in 1691. An assault was led by two guards captains with the grenadier companies of the regiment. Both officers were killed, but the town was captured. Two battalions then returned to France with the King, the other four remaining with the Army of the Marechal-Duc de Luxembourg (4) . The Duc de la Feuillade died at the end of the campaign in 1691 and the honour of commanding the *Gardes Françaises* was conferred on Louis-Francois, Marquis de Boufflers. All battalions were reunited in 1692 when the King was again present to witness the siege of Namur. The following year the regiment was divided again, with two battalions with Louis at the camp at Gemblours and the others at the bloody battle of Neerwinden. The year ended with the guards at the successful siege of Charleroi. In 1694 the guards brigade had the interesting experience of serving under the command of the 'Grand Dauphin' and the last three years of conflict were spent in Flanders in the army of the Duc de Villeroy.

When war broke out in 1701 the *Gardes Françaises* were sent to Brussels to help succour the Spanish Netherlands for the Bourbon claimant Felipe V (Philippe of Anjou, grandson of Louis XIV). Four battalions served at Eckeren, but missed both Villars' early war victories in Germany and the disaster at Blenheim (1704). The Duc de Boufflers had, at this time, been given a company of the *Gardes du Corps* and had relinquished command of the *Gardes Françaises* to the Duc de Guiche. In 1704 the *Gardes Françaises* were serving on the Rhine, but in 1705 returned to Flanders to be present at the siege of Huy. The Duke of Marlborough successfully forced the French lines and broke the siege and the guards brigade, led by its lieutenant colonel, Caraman, was formed into a single body to halt the allies and allow the French army to make its escape. The regiment served at the other three great Marlburian battles of Ramillies, Oudenarde and Malpaquet, but were not present at Villars' great victory at Denain.

GARDES SUISSE

Swiss troops had always served with the armies of the French Crown since the early Italian wars, but like their native guard companions their real origins lie in the French civil wars of the late sixteenth century. The Swiss regiments fought on both sides during the conflict, but it was the Catholic regiment of Pfyffer which became the guard regiment of King Charles IX in 1567. Like the *Gardes Françaises* the regiment assumed various different forms until Henry IV in 1616 adopted a permanent formation under the title 'the Regiment of Swiss Guards'.

Organisation

Throughout this time the *Gardes Suisse* formed four battalions. Like the *Gardes Françaises* they had both pikemen and musketeers during the earlier conflict, but had dispensed with both of these and were flintlock armed during the War of the Spanish Succession. The regiment incorporated, as its senior company, the famous 'Cents-Suisse' of the Kings of France, although they were organised as a separate unit.

Dress

The Swiss Guards were dressed in red after 1661 and from the 1680s adopted blue facings to form a reversal in colouring to the *Gardes Françaises*. Initially their breeches and stockings were red, but these were replaced by blue during the late 1680s. Like the French guard their uniforms were decorated from the 1680s on with white lace.

Marechal de Camp

1. Pierre Stuppa
2. 1701 Maurice Wagner
3. 1702 Francois de Reynold

Captains of the 'Cents-Suisse' (The Hundred Swiss)

1. Jean-Baptise Cassagnet, Marquis de Tilladet
2. 1692 Michel-Francois le Tel lier, Marquis de Courtervaux

Service Record

The regiment served at Walcourt in 1689 and two battalions were at Fleurus the following year. Three battalions were with King Louis at Mons and when the King returned to Versailles one of the battalions accompanied him there. The remaining two battalions played a supporting role in the cavalry attack on the confederate forces at Leuze. Four battalions joined the King at Namur and three were at Steenkirke, where they joined the *Gardes Françaises* in throwing back King William's attempt on Luxembourg's camp. The Swiss were at Neerwinden, where they were held in reserve until the final assault broke the allied line. Like the *Gardes Françaises*, the Swiss were sent in 1701 to succour Felipe V's northern dominions, in particular Brabant. Two companies of grenadiers served at Eckeren in 1703, and 1704 was spent on the Rhine. The *Gardes Suisse* lost very heavily at Ramillies, over 200 casualties being recorded. Finally two battalions were present at both Oudenarde and Malplaquet.

Plate Commentaries

Chapter 5, Part 1

Plate 21

We are fortunate in having Giffart's illustrations as a source for the *Gardes Françaises*. They were published in 1697 and depict the *Gardes* during the later years of the War of the Grand Alliance. Many aspects of their dress are similar to those of other French infantry of the period, so I have drawn regularly from them as a source throughout this series of articles. Despite this, they are still essentially guardsmen and reflect aspects of dress unique to the regiment.

Musketeers, *Gardes Françaises* (top right and left)

In this period the lace on the body was not placed on the cuffs, as was the case later. However on a Eugene Leliepvre reconstruction reproduced in La Sabretache he shows this decoration on the cuffs on the newly formed grenadiers of the regiment. Giffart interestingly shows the firing musketeer in a position suitable only for a man using a rest and impossible otherwise: this probably shows the influence of Lostelnau and other French treatises of the time.

Pikeman, *Gardes Françaises* (centre)

This picture shows clearly the ribbons decorating both shoulders of the guards, modern sources (Leliepvre and Rousselot) are of the opinion that this practice was carried well into the next century. The uniforms of the *Gardes* Reale and Wallon of Felipe V certainly were decorated in this way when they were supplied to the Spanish by the French at the beginning of the succession conflict. Whether this was old stock or possibly designed with the Spanish army specifically in mind are other possibilities. The pikeman is wearing the bright metal cuirass in which the pikes of the guards were deployed until their disbanding.

Ensign, *Gardes Françaises* (bottom left)

The Ensign is seen carrying the Drapeau Colonel (Colonel's colour), of which the regiment had only one. This was carried by the senior battalion along with two blue Drapeaux d'Ordinance. Other battalions would carry three Drapeaux d'Ordinance. Note here the unusual decoration on the ensign's sleeve. Other Giffart plates show horizontal stripes as well as a diagonal pattern.

Sergeant, *Gardes Françaises*

This Sergeant is dressed very plainly with no lace. The text with the plate states that this is campaign dress and therefore a more decorative assembly was presumably worn on special occasions.

Plate 22
Ordnance and Colonel's Colours (top right and left; see notes on Ensign in Plate 21)

Drummer, *Gardes Françaises* (centre)
Drummers of the regiment wore the *Livree du Roi*, as did those of the *Gardes Suisse*. But, whereas the *Gardes Françaises* drummer wears the red breeches and stockings of his regiment, the *Gardes Suisse* drummer would have worn blue. I presume that earlier drummers would have had their coats decorated with ribbons in the manner described above.

Officer, *Gardes Françaises* 1703
The more bizarre forms of decoration are now giving way to a more standardised dress; but this is still, in essence, fashionable clothes in the right colours.

Gardes Françaises 1710
By this time the ribbons have disappeared and the guardsman has taken on a more eighteenth century aspect. The new equipment of a belly pouch and the different positioning of the bayonet (on the left by the sword, rather than on the right by the old style pouch) have now been adopted. In the 1720s the pouch was decorated with a silver edge, but whether this was the case earlier I do not know.

Plate 23
Colonel's and Ordnance Colours (top left and right)
The white colonel's colour in the Swiss regiment was either constructed in separate pieces, or at least stitched along the lines where the decoration of the ordnance flag fell. All comments on the distribution of the flags of the *Gardes Françaises* are relevant here. The colour of the flammes depicted here are only accurate for the period up to 1715, they changed on the accession of Louis XV.

Pikeman, *Gardes Suisse* 1690
The Swiss regiments were notoriously conservative in their dress. In the 1680s the Swiss pikemen were still wearing tassels and shoulder protection, The reduction of the body armour and the retention of the helmet is partly speculative. however it does seem reasonably likely. The decoration at the bottom of the breeches was retained until the early years of the next century.

Gardes Suisse 1710
All comments on the *Gardes Françaises* for this period are relevant here. Now the white lace has been extended to the cuffs.

Officer, *Gardes Suisse* 1710
As above, all references in the details of the *Gardes Françaises* officer are relevant here.

Part Two: The *Garde du Corps* and the Gendarmes and Chevauleger of the Guard

One of the reasons for the success of French arms during the second half of the seventeenth century was the existence of a large reserve of elite cavalry. The cavalry of the Maison du Roi consisted of the four companies of the *Garde du Corps*, single companies of the Gendarmes and Chevauleger, two companies of musketeers and one company of horse grenadiers. The latter three were supposedly usable both on foot and mounted, but it was in the latter manner that they were most often deployed. The musketeers and grenadiers will be covered elsewhere, while this section concentrates on the senior companies of the *Garde du Corps*: the Gendarmes and Chevauleger.

The *Garde du Corps*

There were four companies of *Garde du Corps* (or bodyguards) in existence in 1688. Like the infantry of the Maison du Roi, the *Gardes Françaises* and *Gardes Suisse*, they were not just palace guards and served with the main field armies. They delivered the final blow to the allies' hope at Steenkirk. when the infantry had trodden down enough of the ground to allow cavalry to be used. After 1700 they had their share of defeats: 13 squadrons of the Maison were present at the defeat by the Dutch at Eckeren, and although not heavily engaged a similar number of squadrons were at Oudenarde (at Oudenarde there were also eight squadrons of the Gendarmerie of France, making 21 squadrons of elite cavalry in all).

The first company of *Garde du Corps* was formed in 1440 and was known as the Scottish company. It was formed from a group of Scots in French service under John Stuart, Comte de Boucan (Buchan?) The first captain of the new unit was Robert Patilloch and many of the early captains were Scots. As the prestige of the *Gardes* increased the competition for command of the companies became more intense, indeed even the ranks of the *Gardes* were filled with nobles. By the end of the seventeenth century the captains were all Dukes of the most important houses in France, and normally Marechals also.

The companies and their captains were as follows:

FIRST or SCOTTISH COMPANY (formed 1440)
1678: Anne Jules, Duc de Noailles
1707: Adrien-Maurice, Duc de Noailles

SECOND or FIRST FRENCH COMPANY (formed 1475)
1672: Jacques-Henri de Madam Marquis de Duras
1704: Louis-Francois, Duc de Boufflers
1711: Armand de Bethune, Duc de Charost

THIRD or SECOND FRENCH COMPANY (formed 1479)
1675: Francois-Henri de Montmorency, Duc de Luxembourg
1695: Francois de Neufville, Duc de Villeroi

FOURTH or THIRD FRENCH COMPANY (formed 1516)
1676: Guy-Aldonse de Durfort, Comte de Lorges
1703: Henri, Duc d'Earcourt

Dress and Equipment of the *Garde du Corps*
The dress of the regiment followed the same stylistic changes as described before. Basically broad brimmed hats decorated with feathers and ribbons gave way around the turn of the century to early forms of the tricorn. Likewise the formal raban or cravat became first looser, in the 'Steenkirk' form, and then reduced to a plain stock. The companies also sported bunches of shoulder ribbons in company colours and these dropped out of favour as the tricorn became popular, creating a new 'plainer' look for the beginning of the Spanish Succession conflict. The company colours were worn on the banderole of the carbine, on the pistol holster covers and shabraque, as well as the aforementioned ribbons. Between 1688 and 1715 the company colours were as follows:

> 1st Company: white (holster covers and shabraque red)
> 2nd Company: blue
> 3rd Company: green
> 4th Company: yellow

The coat was dark blue (probably a French Indigo) with red cuffs. Both the body of the coat and the cuffs. as well as the edge of the hat, were decorated with silver lace. The pattern of the lace was regulated in the 1720s but probably had remained much the same for over 20 years, this being borne out by contemporary illustrations of *Garde*s during the 1690s and the early years of the century. Heavy black jacked boots were worn and on campaign soft leather buff gauntlets. The carbine belt was laced in silver. Originally the lace had been positioned around the edge of the banderole, but by the beginning of the period in question a distinctive ladder pattern had been adopted. Likewise the edges of the shabraque and pistol holster cover were decorated with more silver lace, two bands for officers and a single band for the 'humble' guardsmen. Soldiers of the regiment carried two pistols and a carbine. The latter, although carried on the belt when in action was probably 'reversed' and fixed in a 'boot' when on the march. In bad weather a blue cloak, lined in red, was worn. This was carried rolled behind the saddle, with just the lining showing, when not in use.

The Gendarmes and Chevauleger of the Guard
Next in seniority within the cavalry of the Maison came the companies of Gendarmes and Chevauleger. Despite their different titles as far as I can ascertain they were dressed almost identically. Formed originally as cuirassiers during the reign of Henry IV, the Chevauleger company was added later in the manner in which the Gendarmerie of the early sixteenth century had a following of light-horse which supported them by fighting in the successive ranks. At no time however do these Chevauleger seem to have been used in the manner of light horse. Indeed by the time of the

War of the Grand Alliance all of the French regiments of horse were known as Chevauleger, although there was no difference between their dress and equipment and that of the cavalry of the Maison and Gendarmerie.

The Gendarmes and Chevauleger were formed into companies of 200 each and like the *Gardes* du Corps the competition for places in the ranks, commissions and captaincies was intense. The captains were as follows:

GENDARMES
1673: Francois de Rohan, Prince de Soubise
1703: Hercule-Meriadec de Rohan, Prince de Soubise

CHEVAULEGER
1670: N. d'Albert d'Ailly, Duc de Chevreuse
1704: N. d'Albert d'Ailly, Duc de Montfort

Dress and Equipment of the Gendarmes and Chevauleger

In cut and style the dress of these regiments closely resembled that or the *Gardes* du Corps. Likewise the changes occuring during the period 1688–1715 were reflected here. Both regiments wore red coats, heavily decorated in gold lace in the case of the Gendarmes and mixed gold and silver for the Chevauleger. No carbine belt was worn although Guerard's illustration of 1697 shows that at least the Chevauleger carried a carbine. Chartrand in the Osprey Men-at-Arms title lists them as having been equipped with just pistols. Before the beginning of our period the Gendarmes wore black cuffs, but both regiments then appear to have had red cuffs until the Gendarmes had the black reinstated for officers and men (but not NCOs) around 1715.

Plate Commentaries

Chapter 5, Part Two

Plate 24

The two central illustrations show the dress of a guardsman and a musician. Trumpeters and kettle-drummers of the *Garde du Corps* wore coats of a paler blue than the rank and file with red cuffs. Unlike most other Royal regiments the *Gardes* musicians wore silver lace rather than the *livree du Roi*. The lace was placed in vertical bands down the body of the coat and horizontally around the sleeves. The shabraques seem to have been plain blue rather than in the company colour and it appears that no evidence of individual companies colours is present on the uniform. The references that I have for musicians relate to the end of the period, so it may be the case that earlier company colours were worn. however it may also be possible that the musicians were organised centrally and not attached to the companies and this could explain the absence of company colours. The illustration of the officer's coat of 1715 shows the formalised arrangement of the lace which began at this time and stayed much the same until the middle years of the century. Due to the conservative nature of some elements of French military fashion it is reasonable to suppose that officers dressed much the same in the 1690s. There are also illustrations of the company colours as well as two *Gardes* from the 1670s to show the development of the uniform. The trumpet and drum banner were blue with the arms of France and heavily decorated with gold and silver lace.

Standards

The standards of the companies were in the relevant company colours with King Louis' sun in splendour device in the centre in gold with the motto 'NEC PLURIBUS IMPAR' above it on a golden band. Around the edge were decorative embroideries in gold and silver with a fringe of the same. Both sides were the same.

Plate 25

The plate shows the dress of a Gendarme at the time of the Grand Alliance War based on the Guerard illustration with an inset of the coat tail from the same source. The musicians followed the practice of the *Gardes* and didn't wear the *Livree du Roi*. Instead, over a coat of red lined and cuffed in blue, bands of gold lace were worn. Housings and the shabraque were red. By the War of the Spanish Succession officers and NCOs were wearing heavily decorated coats which would remain almost unchanged for 50 years, except for the reintroduction of the black cuffs in 1715. Unfortunately I have been unable to find a reliable reconstruction of the lace of the Chevauleger, so it is not possible to show clearly how their gold and silver lace was arranged.

Standards

The flags of both companies were white with embroidered renderings of clouds and lightning. These were framed in gold with a border of gold and silver decoration. Both sides were identical.

Part Three: The Musketeers and Grenadiers a Cheval

Musketeers (Mousquetaires)

Everybody has surely come across the writings of Alexandre Dumas, transferred, as they have been, on numerous occasions, onto stage and screen. Durnas' novel *The Three Musketeers* is set during the reign of Louis XIII, around the time of the siege of La Rochelle (1628), although Richard Lester's '70s film chose to dress most of the characters in the costume of the 1630s (with apologies for the unfortunate outburst of ex-reenactor's pedantry). Cardinal Richelieu also had a company of musketeers and it was the rivaly between the King's and Cardinal's musketeers that provided the subject matter for Dumas' pen.

The musketeer company formed by Louis XIII in 1622 was disbanded in 1646, but re-formed in 1657 and the second company followed in 1665. Both companies numbered between 250–320 officers and men. They were officially known as the first and second companies 'des Mousquetaires du Roi', but more often as the Gris (Grey) and Noir (Black) from the colour of their horses.

Plate 24

Officer 1st Company c1712

1st Company

2nd Company

Garde c.1694

Trumpeter c.1704

4th Company

Coat and Cuff details

c1675

3rd Company

Garde du Corps
(from Louis XIV in front of the Grotto of Thetis)

Musicians of the *Garde du Corps*
(Illustration by Mark Allen © Wargames Illustrated)
See main text for further information.

Plate 25

Gendarme at the time of the War of the Grand Alliance (based on the Guerard illustration)

(Illustration by Mark Allen © Wargames Illustrated)

See main text for further information.

Plate 26

Musketeers du Roi, 1690–1720

(Illustration by Mark Allen © Wargames Illustrated)

See main text for further information.

Plate 27

Grenadiers à Cheval, 1690–1720
(Illustration by Mark Allen © Wargames Illustrated)
See main text for further information.

Plate 28

French Infantry Regiments
(Illustration by Mark Allen © Wargames Illustrated)
See main text for further information.

Plate 29

French Infantry Regiments
(Illustration by Mark Allen © Wargames Illustrated)
See main text for further information.

Plate 30

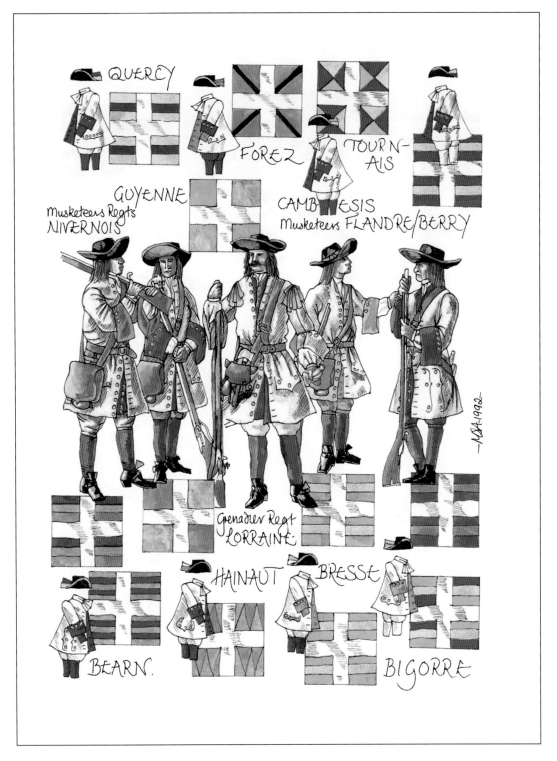

French Infantry Regiments

(Illustration by Mark Allen © Wargames Illustrated)

See main text for further information.

Plate 31

French Infantry Regiments

(Illustration by Mark Allen © Wargames Illustrated)

See main text for further information.

Plate 32

French Infantry Regiments
(Illustration by Mark Allen © Wargames Illustrated)
See main text for further information.

Plate 33

French Colours
(Illustration by Mark Allen © Wargames Illustrated)
See main text for further information.

Plate 34

French Fusilier Regiments
(Illustration by Mark Allen © Wargames Illustrated)
See main text for further information.

Plate 35

French Fusilier Regiments
(Illustration by Mark Allen © Wargames Illustrated)
See main text for further information.

Plate 36

Foreign Troops in French Service

(Illustration by Mark Allen © Wargames Illustrated)

See main text for further information.

Plate 37

Foreign Regiments in French Service
(Illustration by Mark Allen © Wargames Illustrated)
See main text for further information.

Plate 38

Sault/Tesse/Tallard.

Crussol/d'Antin/Gondrin/La Gervaisis

Nettancourt/Mailly/Bueil/LaBrosse/Boufflers

Coetquen/Tourville/Meuse

Humieres/Charost/Bethune/Saillant

General Officers

Fusilier Regt. Tourville/Meuse

Grancey/La Chesnelaye

Drummer Nettancourt

Brendle

St. Sulpice/Lannoy/Louvigny

Vendome/Berry/Barrois

Greder Suisse/Affry

Villars-Chandieu

French Infantry and Colours

Illustration by Mark Allen © Wargames Illustrated

See main text for further information.

Plate 39

French Infantry and Colours
(Illustration by Mark Allen © Wargames Illustrated)
See main text for further information.

Plate 40

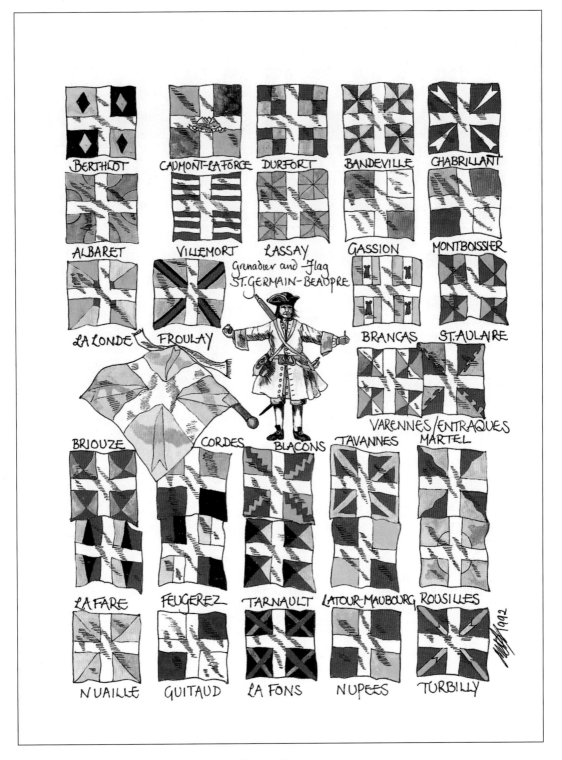

French Colours
(Illustration by Mark Allen © Wargames Illustrated
See main text for further information.

Plate 41

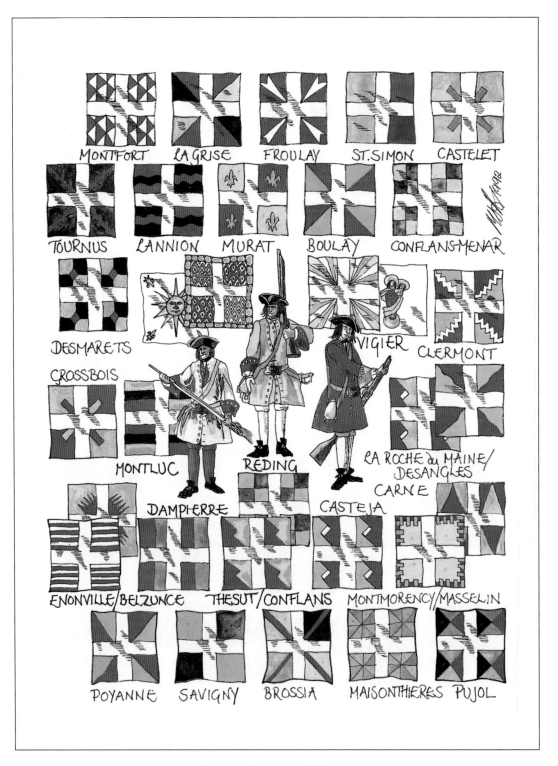

French Infantry and Colours

(Illustration by Mark Allen © Wargames Illustrated)

See main text for further information.

Plate 42

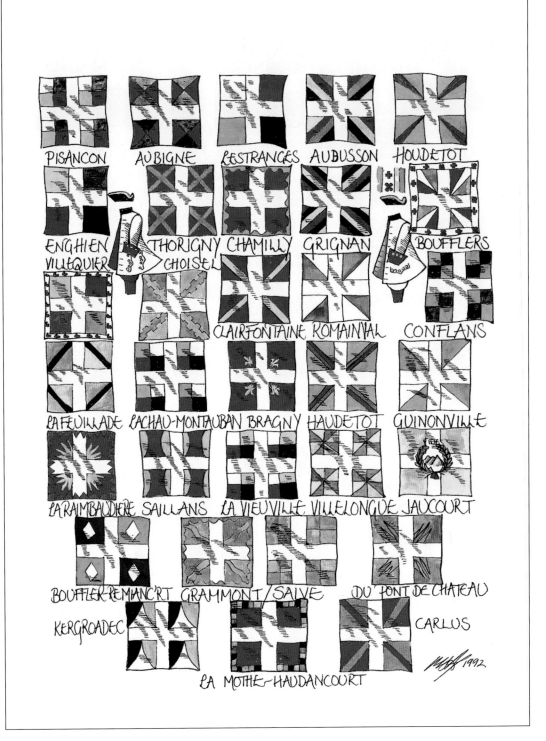

French Colours

(Illustration by Mark Allen © Wargames Illustrated)

See main text for further information.

Plate 43

French Colours
(Illustration by Mark Allen © Wargames Illustrated)
See main text for further information.

The companies and their captains were as follows:

First or Grey Company
1657: Philippe Mancini, Duc de Nevers
1667: Charles de Bats-Castelmor, Comte d'Artaignan (allegedly the historical character upon whom Dumas based his own d'Artaignan. He was killed leading as an assault at the siege of Maastricht in 1673, during the Dutch War).
1673: Louis de Forbin
1684: Louis de Melun de Maupertuis
1716: Louis de Montesquiou, Comte d'Artaignan

Second or Black Company
1665: Edouard-Francois Colbert de Maulevrier
1672: Francois de Montbaron, Comte de Tourvoye
1674: Jean de *Garde* d'Agoult, Marquis de Vins
1716: Jean de Montboissier-Beaufort

Organisation, Dress and Equipment of the Musketeers
A company musketeers generally consisted of: one capitaine-lieutenant, two sous-lieutenants, two ensignes and two comettes, 10 marechaux-de-logis, two aides-majors de brigade, one porte-etendard, one porte-drapeau, one fourrier, six drummers and four hautbois (musicians were mounted on greys whatever the company), and 198 musketeers. The numbers in a company could vary considerably from time to time.

From their formation in the 1620s the Musketeers of the King had worn blue tabards with a white cross and edging, whilst the Cardinal's household wore red with a white cross and red and white edging. When the new companies were formed the blue tabard was retained and the cross was differenced to allow the members of each company to be recognised. The plate on the musketeers shows the different crosses prescribed. The tabard grew longer as the century progressed till in the 1680s it became a long cape-like garment, totally impractical in combat. So in 1685 the tabard was replaced for 'day to day' wear by a sleeveless *soubreveste*, which is shown being worn in all the plates. As mounted infantry the musketeer companies were accompanied by both trumpeters and drummers, the *soubrevestes* of musicians being particularly heavily decorated with lace. Likewise the *soubrevestes* of the regiment's brigadiers (NCOs) were supplied around the edge with extra lace. Officers did not wear the *soubreveste*.

Originally the members of the companies wore only the tabard to distinguish them, wearing their own clothes underneath, however in 1673 uniforms were adopted. The companies wore red coats like the Gendarmes of the Guard, with gold decoration for the first company and gold and silver for the second (in 1716 the second company adopted silver decorations). These colourings were also reflected in the horse furniture (see Plate 26). According to Rene Chartrand, during the 1680s the companies wore blue or green knots of ribbon on the shoulders and cuffs of their red coats, the practice dying away in the 1690s. Chartrand also suggests that hat plumes were white and crimson during the early years, standardising on white by the late 1670s. The cut of the coat followed the general trend of the period with a straight cut style with tight sleeves and the aforementioned ribbons giving way to a looser style gather at the rear with much wider sleeves towards the end of Louis XIV's reign. Officers' coats were heavily decorated with lace, the position of the lace being standardised in the early years of the eighteenth century and lasting until the reforms which followed in the wake of the disastrous Seven Years' War. Whilst, as mentioned above, the musicians' *soubreveste* was heavily laced, their coat was plain red. According to Chartrand the Musketeers originally carried matchlock muskets, superceded during the 1660s by flintlock carbines.

The Grenadiers du Roi

The last of the companies of cavalry of the 'Maison du Roi' to be formed, the Grenadiers a Cheval de la *Garde* were raised in 1676 at the end of the campaign of that year. Susane (*Histoire de la Cavalerie Francaise*) says they were 'destined to march into combat at the head of the cavalry of the Maison to open the way and clear the passage for the corps'. As the company was recruited from amongst the 'bravest infantry grenadiers' I have always had an image of the way being blocked by all the infantry grenadiers who have fallen off their horses. However as their reputation is that of the 'elite of the elite', they must have received suitable training in horsemanship. The company was also used, along with the musketeers, in a dismounted role. This was often the case at sieges where the 'Rol Soleil' would turn up to watch the progress.

The captains of the company were as follows:

> 1676: N. de Villemeur, Marquis de Riotor
> 1691: Francois, Marquis de Villemeur
> 1730: Jean-Francois de Nancre, Marquis de Creil

Organisation, Dress and Equipment

The numbers of Grenadiers varied: 92 officers and men in 1676, 120 in 1678, 100 in 1679, 168 in 1690, 250 in 1696, and 84 in 1725. Susane details the company as follows: one capitaine-lieutenant, three lieutenants, three sous-lieutenants, three marechaux-de-logis, six sergeants, three brigadiers, six sous-brigadiers, one porte-etendard, two fourriers, six appointes (these are, I presume, officers serving in the ranks), four drummers and 130 grenadiers.

On their formation the Grenadiers adopted red laced coats with white 'loops' as decoration. They wore a brown fur hat with a red hanging bag. There is an excellent illustration of an early grenadier in Rene Chartrand's Men-at-Arms title, *Louis XIV's Army*. In 1692 blue coats were issued. Chartrand says 'the coat did not have loops as yet, but was edged with narrow silver lace until around 1730'. Chartrand's description accords with the Delaitre illustrations of 1721. But Delaitre shows the waistcoat decorated with a thin edge of silver lace, whilst a review of 1698 says, 'they have red waistcoats with large loops'. Eugene Leliepvre's reconstruction, on which I have based my central illustration, shows no lace on the coat. It seems to have its origins in a plate by Geurard dating from the end of the war of the Grand Alliance depicting a mounted 'flying Grenadier' hurling a grenade. As no other mounted grenadiers existed in the army at this time it may safely be assumed that this is a Grenadier de la *Garde*. No lace can be seen on the coat. The musicians wore the company coat heavily decorated with the 'Tyree du Roi' lace, the drum being plain blue with the royal arms. In the Geurard illustration, mentioned above, the cap has a plain hanging bag. By the time of the Delaitre plates this has been replaced by a more elaborate design. When the change took place is difficult to ascertain, however, like the standardised ranking system shown on Plate 27, it is quite possible that it was in place during the latter years of Louis XIV's reign. The Grenadiers were equipped with a curved sabre, two pistols and a flintlock carbine.

Part 4: French Infantry, Uniforms and Equipment

Before going on to the specific items of regimental uniforms it would be useful to give a general view of French infantry clothing at this time. Most articles listed below would be universal to armies of the period.

Hat

A low crowned felt hat was worn by all French infantry. Even grenadiers, who in other armies were given specialist headwear, wore the hat in French service. By this time the hat was normally black, although brown and grey had been common earlier in the King's reign. Grenadiers had begun the practice of pinning or tying up two or more sides, to make the task of throwing grenades easier, and this may have been the origination of the tricorn. How general the wearing of the hat in the tricorn fashion had become is difficult to ascertain, the engravings of Guerard which date from the last years of the century and depict soldiers during the Grand Alliance Wars show all the enlisted men wearing a form of tricorn. On the other hand the illustrations of the *Gardes Françaises* by Giffart (1696) show no tricorns except amongst the NCOs and officers. The irony here is that Guerard's officers are not wearing tricorns. However there is some common ground in that in both series the tricorns shown are of a large 'improvised' type, i.e. they are large felt hats turned into tricorns rather than hats manufactured specifically as tricorns.

Shirt

A full linen shirt of a standard late-seventeenth century type would be worn. It would be cut without a yoke and the sleeves would be gathered into a plain band at the cuffs. Attachments would be by ties or buttons. At the neck the soldier would have worn, in most cases, a short plain scarf or rabat of off-white cloth. Later black was adopted by many regiments and often worn reversed.

Coat and Vest

A full coat of grey serge was worn with a system of regimental differencing using coloured cuffs, breeches, hose and vests. The vest was a sleeved waistcoat worn under the coat. Because the coat sleeves were slightly shorter than the sleeves of the vest, the vest was exposed at the cuffs. Information on the position and shape of pockets, number and colour of buttons, etc., is difficult to come by, so in producing the detailed examination of regimental dress I have tried to give the most likely colours. It is worth noting that in the British army of this period a soldier's vest was made up from his old coat when it was replaced; whether this occurred across the Channel I don't know. Rene Chartrand noted in his articles in *Military Modelling* (December 1986 and October 1987) on early French infantry that the French were slow to supply their men with vests, not doing so completely until the early 1690s. Finally many coats of this era were still worn with bunches of ribbons attached to one or both sleeves. Where the colours are known I have illustrated them. Many more regiments probably wore them, but the colours are unknown. The practice had, in general, died out by 1700.

Breeches, Hose and Shoes
The breeches of this period were cut tighter than earlier seventeenth century styles with the exception of the Swiss who, according to Rene Chartrand, wore 'baggy breeches' decorated at the bottoms with 'ribbon-points'. Hose or stockings were often coloured and long enough to have the tops pulled over the bottoms of the breeches when tied at the knee. Shoes were normally plain black with tin buckles.

Weapons and Equipment
It is not my intention to discuss at great length the weapons of the 'lantassin' during Louis' wars, however, certain general information is necessary to complete the picture. Although slow to recognise the advantages of the flintlock mechanism, when the French began to re-equip the process was completed more rapidly than in many other armies. After 1692 the process to re-arm was accelerated so that seven years later the matchlock had been officially abandoned. Two years later the 'queen of the battle' was finally given up and pikemen no longer were part of a French regiment of foot. During the Grand Alliance period the pikemen appear to have still been equipped with a back- and breast-plate as protection although unlike the Swiss regiments in French service they had given up the wearing of helmets. The musketeers of the French army were issued with a waist belt on which was carried a short infantry hanger with a brass hilt. Over the left shoulder went a belt carrying the ammunition pouch and powder flask together with the socket bayonet, which began to be introduced in the mid 1690s (the earlier plug bayonet was carried on the waist belt over the sword frog). The French ammunition pouch was of distinctly different style to those of other nations and is illustrated below.

Drummers
French infantry regiments can be split into three categories. Firstly Royal regiments who had the King as their colonel and whose drummers and other musicians would wear the King's livery or *Livree du Roi*. Secondly there were regiments who took their name from a province and likewise used the *Livree du Roi*. Finally came the rest of the regiments whose colonelcies could be bought and sold and whose drummers wore the liveries of their respective colonels.

Colours

Each French infantry battalion fielded three colours, the senior battalion carried the white colonel's colour. After the Battle of Fleurus in 1689 a white scarf began to be carried atop the standard pole.

The French Infantry Regiments

PICARDIE (red colours to the left of figure, Plate 28)
Mestres de Camp:
    1677 Henri, Duc d'Harcourt
    1691 Louis de Melun, Prince d'Epinoy
Drummers: *Livree du Roi*

PIEMONT (black colours to the left of figure, Plate 28)
Mestres de Camp:
    1680 Claude de Faverges, Marquis de Rebe d'Arques
    1693 Paul de Montmorency, Duc de Chatillon
Drummers: *Livree du Roi*.
Officers and sergeants: black velvet cuffs

NAVARRE (brown decorated colours to the left of figure, Plate 28)
Mestres de Camp:
    1683 Francois de la Rochefoucaud, Duc de la Rocheguyon
    1696 Francois Colberg, Marquis de Maulevrier
Drummers: *Livree du Roi*. The badge illustrated is the arms of the Kingdom of Navarre depicted on the colours of the regiment.

CHAMPAGNE (green colours to the left of figure, Plate 28)
Mestres de Camp:
    1689 Charles Colbert, Comte de Sceaux
    1690 Jules-Armand Colbert, Marquis de Blainville
Drummers: *Livree du Roi*

NORMANDIE (yellow colours to the right of figure, Plate 28)
Mestres de Camp:
    1674 Louis, Comte de Guisard
    1691 Jean-Georges de Guisard, Comte de la Bonnie
Drummers: *Livree du Roi*

LA MARINE (green and blue colours to the right of figure, Plate 28)
Mestres de Camp:
    1683 Henri de la Rochefoucaud, Marquis de Tonnay-Charente
    1694 Louis-Jean Charles, Marquis de Talleyrand
Drummers: *Livree du Roi*

BOURBONNAIS (violet and blue colours to the right of figure, Plate 28)
Mestre de Camp:
    1687 Louis-Pierre-Armand d'Aloigny, Marquis de Rochefort

Drummers: *Livree du Roi*

FEUQUIERES (yellow and violet colours to the right of figure, Plate 28)
Mestres de Camp:
    1689 Jules de Pas, Marquis de Feuquieres
Drummers: unknown
Colours from P. Charrie, *Drapeaux et Etandards du Roi*. Note: the regiment Richelieu during the Spanish Succession Wars carried the same colours.

AUVERGNE (violet and black colours above figure with violet vest, Plate 28)
Mestres de Camp:
    1680 Nicolas de Nicolais, Marquis de Presles
    1695 Claude-Francois de Boutellier, Marquis de Chavigny
Drummers: *Livree du Roi*

SAULT (grey, yellow and black colours well above and to the right of figure, (Plate 28)
Mestre de Camp:
    1681 Jean-Francois-Paul de Blachefort de Bonne de Crequi, Comte de Sault
Drummers: unknown
Colours from Charrie

VAUBECOURT/NETTANCOURT (violet & red colours to the left of figure, Plate 28)
Mestres de Camp:
    1677 Louis-Claude de Nettancourt Haussonville, Comte de Vaubecourt
    1695 Louis, Marquis de Nettancourt Haussonville
Drummers: unknown

LE ROI (red and green colours with fleur-de-lys to the left of figure, Plate 28)
Mestres de Camp:
    1678 Gaston-Jean-Baptiste de Mornay, Comte de Montchevreuil
    1693 Louis-Charles d'Hautefort, Marquis de Surville
Drummers: *Livree du Roi*.
Inset: grenadier's pocket

ROYAL (brown and violet colours with fleur-de-lys to left of figure, Plate 28)
Mestres de Camp:
    1680 Francois-Joseph de Blachefort, Marquis de Crequi
    1693 Benoit, Marquis de Calvo
Drummers: *Livree du Roi*

LYONNAIS (black and blue colours directly below figure, Plate 28)
Mestre de Camp:
    1683 Louis-Nicolas de Neufville, Marquis d'Alincourt
Drummers: Livree du Maison Villeroi (Regiment Lyonnais was the only Provincial regiment allowed to use a different livery to the *Livree du Roi*;

this was because the regiment was owned by the Neufville family, Dukes of Villeroi). The drums were green and carried the Villeroi crest. Cross worn on the back and front of drummers' coats.

POITOU (red and blue colours to the left of figure, Plate 28)
Mestre de Camp:
   1689 Leonor de Montchevreuil, Comte de Mornay
Drummers: *Livree du Roi*

LE DAUPHIN (single figure without colours at bottom of Plate 28)
Mestre de Camp:
   1671 Marquis de Beringhen
Drummers: *Livree du Roi.* Wagner (*Bernalungsangaben fue zeit des Spanischen Erbfolge Krieges 1701–14*) gives the regiment blue coats with orange lace; but Lucien Rousselot (I feel a more reliable source) lists *Livree du Roi* with blue drums and the Dauphin's arms (inset). Dauphin's colours are depicted on a larger scale as Illustration 1 with the colonel's colour shown above and the Ordonnance colour below.

CRUSSOL (bottom right hand corner of Plate 28, colours to right)
Mestres de Camp:
   1687 Louis, Duc de Crussol d'Uzes
   1693 Jean-Charles, Duc de Crussol d'Uzes
Drummers: wite coats, red facings, and silver lace (Chartrand etc.)

TOURRAINE (yellow, blue, green and red colour to right of figure, Plate 28)
Mestres de Camp:
   1680 Jean deBonnac, Marquis d'Usson
   1691 Nicolas de Courchamp, Comte d'Igny
Drummers: *Livree du Roi*

ANJOU (single figure next to Tourraine, see Plate 28)
Mestre de Camp: 1681 Francois-Marie, Comte de Hautefort
Drummers: *Livree du Roi.*
Colours shown larger scale as Illustration 3. Colonel's colour below, Ordonnance colour above.

TURENNE (figure with black colours with tower to the right, Plate 28)
Mestre de Camp:
   1679 Henri d'Harcourt, Marquis de Thury
Drummers: unknown (could be the same as the Colonel-General's Cavalry which wore the Turenne Livery, if so see section on French horse regiments).

d'HUMIERES (green colours with white squares, figure to the left, Plate 29)
Mestre de Camp: 1689 Louis-Francois d'Aumont, Duc d'Humieres
Drummers: Aumont Livery (from Eugene Leliepvre illustrations of d'Humieres' regiment of horse. Cross shown was worn on the back and front of drummer's coat.

GUICHE/NOAILLES/COETQUEN (green and violet colours, figure to the left, Plate 29)
Mestres de Camp:
  1687 Antoine de Grammont, Comte de Guiche
  1693 Anne-Jules, Duc de Noailles
  1696 Malo-August, Marquis de Coetquen
Second illustration is of the uniform as Noailles, when the yellow cuffs were dropped. The yellow vest is speculative, but vest was yellow in 1709 as the Marquis de Tourville's Regiment (red cuffs as Tourville's).
Drummers: unknown

GRANCEY (red and black colours, figure to the left, Plate 29)
Mestres de Camp:
  1675 Jacques-Leonor de Medavy, Comte de Grancey
  1693 Francois Rouxel de Medavy, Marquis de Grancey
Drummers: unknown

LIMOUSIN (green, yellow and red colours, figure to the left, Plate 29)
Mestre de Camp:
  1684 Louis de la Palud de Bouligneux, Comte de Meilly
Drummers: unknown

LA REINE (green and black colours with fleur-de-lys, figure below, Plate 29)
Mestres de Camp:
  1688 Michel-Francois Le Tellier, Marquis de Courtenvaux
  1691 Rene de Froulay, Comte de Tesse
  1693 Louis d'Ornaison, Marquis de Buzancois
Drummers: red coats, blue cuffs. Queen's livery as shown, white line on blue background. Lace would have covered the body of the coat down the seam lines and be arranged horizontally around the arms. Red drum.
Colours: gold crowns and fleur-de-lys.

ROYAL des VAISSEAUX (yellow, red, green and black colours slightly below and to the right of figure, Plate 29)
Mestres de Camp:
  689 Louis, Comte de Mailly
  1692 Rene, Marquis de Nevet
Drummers: *Livree du Roi*

ORLEANS (figure at right hand bottom of page with blue and brown colours above and to the left, Plate 29)
Mestre de Camp:
  1684 Claude-Alexis, Comte de Bailleul
Drummers: coat as La Reine, livery lace Orleans as illustrated

LA COURONNE (blue colours with crown to the left of figure, Plate 29)
Mestres de Camp:
  1637 Hardouin Bruslart, Chevalier de Genlis

1693 Nicolas de Prunier, Marquis de Saint-Andrew
Drummers: *Livree du Roi*. Later in the eighteenth century the words 'DEDIT HANC MASTREKA CORONAM'.

BRETAGNE (orange and black decorated colours above and to left of figure, Plate 29)
Mestre de Camp:
   1683 Louis-Anne-Jules Potier, Marquis de Novion
Drummers: *Livree du Roi*
Colours: the black devices depicted on the Ordonnance colours are the heraldic symbol for ermine and also appear on the arms of Brittany on the colonel's colour.

SOISSONS/PERCHE (red and blue colours. Above figure, in bottom left corner, Plate 29)
Mestres de Camp:
   1665 Henri de Chapelas, Comte de Salieres
   1690 Joseph de Robert, Marquis de Lignerac
Drummers: (as Perche) Livres du Roi

ARTOIS (yellow and blue colours to the right of figure, Plate 29)
Mestres de Camp:
   1675 Francois-Gaston de l'Hotel, Marquis d'Escots
   1690 Nicolas, Marquis d'Escots
   1692 Nicolas-Simon Arnauld, Marquis de Pomponne
Drummers: *Livree du Roi*

LA CHARTRE (red and blue colours below figure, Plate 29)
Mestre de Camp:
   1684 Louis-Charles-Edme, Marquis de la Chartre
Drummers: as Orleans, but with plain silver lace
Colours from Charrie

VENDOME (two large figures in centre of Plate 29, colours depicted above grenadier's head)
Mestre de Camp:
   1669 Louis-Joseph, Duc de Vendome
Drummers: unknown
The two figures are based on Giffart plates and depict a junior officer and a grenadier.

Plate 30

QUERCY
Mestres de Camp:
   1684 N. de La Queile, Marquis d'Amanze (killed defending Embrun, in the Alps against the Duke of Savoy)
   1689 Claude-Francois, Chevalier de Bouthillier

Drummers: *Livree du Roi*

Flag: violet and yellow stripes. This shows the problem of using Funcken as the only source. *The Lace Wars* Part 1 shows the violet section of the flag as a sort of 'off black', Charrie however makes the matter much clearer.

TOURNAISIS
Mestres de Camp:
   1684 Marquis de Broilly
   16?? Omer Pucelle d'Orgemont
Drummers: *Livree du Roi*
Flag: red and yellow stripes

FOREZ or FOREST
Mestres de Camp:
   1684 Jean-Noel de Barbezieres, Comte de Chemerauft
   1693 N. Comte de Montmorency-Fosseuse (killed at Marsaglia)
   1693 Louis, Marquis de Polastron
Drummers: Wagner lists blue coat with red and white lace, I have shown a possible interpretation on Plate 32. However it is also possible, indeed more likely in fact, that *Livree du Roi* was worn.
Flag: aurore (a sort of French salmon pink) with a black saltire.

CAMBRESIS
Mestres de Camp:
   1684 N. Comte de Chateaurenaud (wounded at Staffarde)
   1693 Charles-Louis-Anne, Comte de Montberon
   1694 N. de Vienne, Marquis de Presles
Drummers: *Livree du Roi*
Flag: descriptions in Charrie and the Funckens agree, on this occasion. However *The Lace Wars* shows a rotation in the design which is not mentioned in Charrie nor does it completely make sense in itself. To make sense of the pattern green should be on the right in 3 and on the top in 4.

GUYENNE
Mestre de Camp:
   1684 Charles de la Rochefoucauld, Comte de Blanzac
Drummers: *Livree du Roi*
Flag: Isabelle (a browny-yellow) and grey-green. *The Lace Wars* lists the flag that was carried from 1762 (crimson and violet) as being in use from 1684, however the flag illustrated is correct not only for this period but also up to the regiment's disbandment during the Seven Years' War.

LORRAINE
Mestres de Camp:
   1684 N. de Monchy, Marquis d'Hocquincourt (killed at Fleunis)
   1689 Comte d'Hocquincourt, brother of the above (killed at d'Huy)
   1692 Jean-Marie Percin, Marquis de Montgalliard
Drummers: *Livree du Roi*

Flag: pale green and grey-de-lin (mauve). Funcken shows the mauve as grey.

FLANDRE
Mestre de Camp:
    1684 N. le Sens, Marquis de Folleville
Drummers: *Livree du Roi*
Flag: blue and yellow stripes

BERRY
Mestre de Camp:
    1684 Louis-Vincent de Budes, Marquis de Goesbriant (mortally wounded
    at Castelnuovo de Bormia 1702)
Drummers: *Livree du Roi*
Flag: violet and Isabelle stripes. Funcken shows the brown too dark and the
violet as an even darker area of brown.

BEARN
Mestres de Camp:
    1684 Charles-Henri de Mornay, Marquis de Montchevreuil (killed at
    Mannheim during the invasion of the Palatinate in 1688)
    1688 Leonor, Comte de Mornay (brother of the above)
    1689 Francois Bouton, Chevalier de Chamilly (killed at Friedlingen 1702)
Drummers: *Livree du Roi*
Flag: Isabelle and red stripes.

NANAULT
Mestres de Camp:
    1684 Nicholas-Simon Arnaud, Marquis de Pomponne
    1692 N. de Morstein, Comte de Chateauvilain (killed at defense of Namur)
    1695 Henri-Antoine de Ricouard, Marquis de Herouville
Drummers: *Livree du Roi*
Flag: blue and aurore triangles

BIGORRE
Mestre de Camp:
    1684 Etienne-Gerard Pellot, Chevalier de Trevieres
Drummers: *Livree du Roi*
Flag: green, yellow, and red stripes

BRESSE
Mestre de Camp:
    1684 Rene-Alexis Le Senechal, Comte de Kerado-Molac
Drummers: *Livree du Roi*
Flag: green and yellow stripes.

Plate 31

LA MARCHE
Mestre de Camp:
   1684 Armand-Charles de Gortout, Baron de Biron
Drummers: *Livree du Roi*
Flag: blue, red and brown with yellow horizontals

NIVERNAIS or NIVERNOIS
Mestres de Camp:
   1684 Paul-Sigismond de Montmorency-Luxembourg, Comte de Luxe
   1689 Elie de Castelmoron, Comte de Belzunce
Drummers: *Livree du Roi*
Flag: brown, blue and Isabelle stripes. *The Lace Wars* shows only brown and blue

BRIE
Mestres de Camp:
   1684 Armand de Bethune, Marquis de Charost
   1690 Antoine-Alexandre de Canouville, Marquis de Raffetot
Drummers: *Livree du Roi*
Flag: red with a yellow saltire

SOISSONAIS
Mestres de Camp:
   1684 N. de Goyon-Grimaldi. Duc de Valentinois
   1696 Charles d'Ambly, Marquis de Chaumont
Drummers: *Livree du Roi*
Flag: blue with a yellow saltire

ISLE DE FRANCE
Mestres de Camp:
   1684 Antoine-Louis de Pardaillon-Gondrin, Marquis d'Antin
   1689 Henri Ambroux, Comte de la Massays
Drummers: *Livree du Roi*
Flag: reconstructed from Charrie this one could be completely wrong. The yellow may be horizontal or vertical or may even go diagonally the other way!

VEXIN
Mestre de Camp:
   1684 Pierre d'Hautefort, Comte de Montignac
Drummers: *Livree du Roi*
Flag: black and yellow with 'dog-toothed' edging

AUNTS
Mestre de Camp:
   1684 Armand-Sidoine-Apollinaire Gaspard, Vicomte de Polignac
   (wounded at Friedlingen 1702)
Drummers: *Livree du Roi*

Flag: green and red triangles separated by a Isabelle saltire. Again Funcken shows the Isabelle as brown.

BEAUCE
Mestre de Camp:
    1684 N. de Pompadour, Marquis de Lauriere
Drummers: *Livree du Roi*
Flag: black and blue with 'lightning' edging.

DAUPHINE
Mestre de Camp:
    1684 Sebastien-Hyacinthe le Senechal, Chevalier de Kerado-Molac
Drummers: *Livree du Roi*
Flag: red, green and brown

VIVARAIS
Mestres de Camp:
    1684 N. Marquis de Breute
    1685 Jacques le Coutellier, Marquis de Saint-Pater
Drummers: *Livree du Roi*
Flag: another reconstruction of Charrie. Both the red and green on the original flag had aurore threads mixed in the material, this caused the flag to give a 'shimmery' effect. *The Lace Wars* again shows the post-1762 flag.

LUXEMBOURG
Mestres de Camp:
    1684 N. de Brancas, Duc de Villars
    1694 Vicomte de Comblizy
Drummers: *Livree du Roi*
Flag: yellow and black stripes

BASSIGNY
Mestres de Camp:
    1684 Louis, Comte de Mailly
    1692 Jules-Auguste Potier, Marquis de Gesvres
Drummers: *Livree du Roi*
Flag: The green and red areas on this flag were prepared in the same way as those on Vivarais (see above).

BEAUJOLAIS
Mestre de Camp:
    1684 Jean-Thomas, Marquis de Berulle
Drummers: *Livree du Roi*
Flag: gironne pattern of green and red

Plate 32

PONTHIEU
Mestres de Camp:
1685 Florent de Chatelet, Comte de Lomont
1697 Claude, Marquis de Ceberet
Drummers: *Livree du Roi*
Flag: aurore with a green 'dog-toothed' saltire

NOAILLES
Mestres de Camp:
   1689 Anne-Jules, Duc de Noailles
   1691 Incorporated into Noailles' other regiment (see below)
Drummers: unknown, probably based on the family armourial colours of crimson/red and yellow.
Flag: crimson with a dark yellow saltire

TESSE
Mestre de Camp:
   1689 Rene de Froulay, Comte de Tesse
Drummers: unknown.
Flag: mauve with a yellow and black saltire

NOAILLES
Formed in 1691 all other details as above

GATINOIS
Mestre de Camp:
   1692 Henri. Vicomte de Poudenx
Drummers: *Livree du Roi*
Flag: black with a yellow and green saltire

BARROIS
Mestre de Camp:
   1692 Louis Desmoulins, Comte de Lisle
Drummers: *Livree du Roi*
Flag: Isabelle and red. Barrois flag is actually the flag of the successor regiment Conti. Barrois flag is unknown.

BLAISOIS
Mestre-de-Camp: 1692 Henri de la Tour d'Auvergne, Comte d'Evreux
Drummers: Livree du Roi
Flag: red and blue with a broken yellow diagonal (see above).

AUXERROIS
Mestre-de-Camp: 1692 N. Comte de Vaissieux
Drummers: Livree du Roi
Flag: red, blue and yellow

AGENOIS
Mestre de Camp:
    1692 Antoine Cleriadus, Comte de Choiseul-Beaupre
Drummers: Wagner gives the drummers yellow coats (violet lace?) but *Livree du Roi* is a more likely option as Agenois was a provincial regiment.
Flag: yellow and violet.

SANTERRE
Mestre de Camp:
    1692 Louis-Francois-Henri de Colbert, Chevalier de Croissy
Drummers: *Livree du Roi*
Flag: Green and brown with a 'dog-toothed' edging

DES LANDES
Mestre de Camp: 1693 Adrien, Comte de Mailly de Housaye
Drummers: as in the case of Agenois Wagner lists yellow coats (red lace?) and again *Livree du Roi* seems the more likely.

As you will see from Plate 33, information on the dress of these particular regiments is pretty scarce with only one regiment, Sourches, having any details at all. Even in the case of this regiment the accuracy of the information is highly questionable and almost certainly applies to the regiment that the Marechal de Camp Louis de Bouchet de Sourches, Comte de Montserreau commanded from 1703–6 rather than the two different regiments he led between 1690 and 1697. However, it is just possible that elements of the dress of the earlier regiments were worn later and without any details on the other regiments it is nice to have something on one of them, however speculative.

Many of the units listed below have a place name in brackets following their date of formation. This shows that they were formed from the local militia of that area. This was a measure taken by the French to free more front line troops for the field armies. These new regiments for the most part replaced the better quality troops in garrison duties, although some did see action: CAVOYE, Siege of Ath; HERBOUVILLE, Charleroi and Neerwinden; LA GARDE, Defence of Namur; MONTENAY, Neerwinden; VILLARS, Neerwinden; DULAC, Staffarde; LAUNAY, Neerwinden. Whilst uniform details are scarce, flag details are relatively plentiful. Most illustrations are reconstructions from Charrie (*Drapeaux et Etendards du Roi*, Paris 1989) with the aid of a French heraldry book, so must be looked at in that context. I hope for the most part that they are pretty accurate, but I am sure that errors will have crept in.

Further Notes on the Use of Livery and Lace
Plate 34 shows a drummer of the Languedoc Regiment in a blue coat with red facings and a strip of red and white lace, greatly enlarged running vertically up from the drawing of the coat. This represents the King's Livery, or *Livree du Roi*, worn by drummers in most French regiments of infantry at this time. The basic blue and red coat was liberally adorned with the lace, often in the style shown in the illustration.

Lyonnais: The green and aurore (a sort of slightly pinky French orange) coat of the Villeroi liveried regiment was decorated in similar style to the above with parallel lines of gold and aurore lace. Lyonnais drummers had, in addition, a white cross, edged aurore with fleur-de-lys of the same, on the breasts and backs of their coats. These white crosses, the ancient symbol of France, were probably used by many more regiments, including those wearing the *Livree du Roi*, but I have no specific details. It is worth noting at this point that in all the illustrations that I have seen the drummers wearing the *Livree du Roi* wear the same colour breeches and stockings as other soldiers of their regiment.

It is my opinion, contrary to sources such as Wagner's *Bernalungsangaben fur zeit des Spardschen Erbfolge Krieges 1701–14* that the vast majority of regiments wearing the *Livree du Roi* had blue drums.

The lace on the coat of the drummer of the regiment d'Humieres is displayed in a less obtrusive way than those already described. The drawing was based on a reconstructed cavalry trumpeter of the cavalry regiment of the same name. It is therefore possible that the information relates directly to the cavalry regiment d'Humieres and that the lace on the drummers' coats worn by the infantry regiment would have horizontal sleeve lace like those already covered.

To the best of my knowledge both regiments La Reine (Queen's) and Orleans, in general appear to follow the trends covered already. The Orleans coat of arms pictured here was also illustrated on the drums of the regiment. I have no further information on the La Chartre regiment.

The Regiments

Listed below are the regiments, the name of the first Marechal de Camp is on the line below the regiment's name. Any further changes of commanding officer are listed with the date of the changeover.

Merode/Tournon (1688)
N. de Gand-Vilain Comte de Merode
1690 Louis de Pasquier de Tournon

Cavoye/Mouchy (1689) (d'Amiens)
Gilbert Oger de Cavoye
1695 N. de Noailles, Comte de Mouchy

La Ilhiere (1689) (Soissons)
Louis de Polastron de la llhiere
Herbouville (1689) (Rouen) Adrien Comte d'Herbouville

La *Garde*/Villiers (1689) (Caen)
N. Baron de la *Garde*
1695 N. de Villiers

Montenay (1689) (d'Alençon)
N. de Montenay

Menou (1689) (Orleans)
Charles Baron Menou

Villars (1689) (Moulins)
N. Marquis de Villars

Cottanges (1689) (d'Auvergne)
N. de Cottanges

Desmoulins (1689) (Limoges)
N. de Desmoulins, Comte d'Arginy

Aligny (1689) (Dijon)
Pierre Quaure d'Aligny

Vaugrenant (1689) (Franche Comte)
N. Feting de Vaugrenant

Du Guast/d'Argenson (1689) (Grenoble)
N. de Berayer du Guast
1695 N. d'Argenson

Caixon (1689) (Montauban)
Jean de Caixon

Poudenx/La Bastide (1689) (Bordeaux)
Henri Vicomte de Poudenx
1692 N. de La Bastide

Bonivatel (1689) (Perigord)
N. de Bonivatel

Boulins (1689) (Bayonne)
N. de Boulins

Boissieres (1689) (d'Agen)
N. Marquis de Durfort-Boissierres

Saint-Jai (1689) (Reims)
N. de St. Tal

Dulac (1689) (Dauphine)
N. Dulac

Launay (1689) (Anjou)
N. de Launay

Fontenay (1689) (Flandre)

N. de Fontenay

Lignery (1689) (Mans)
N. de Lignery

Dupas (1689) (d'Arras)
N. Dupas

Lignieres (1689) (Chateauroux)
N. de Lignieres

Du Moulin/Marcilly (1689) (d'Autun)
N. de Moulin
Achille Poulet Marquis de Marcilly

Bellisle (1689) (Bretagne)
Francois Peiroi de Bellisle

Berville (1689) (Creil)
N. de Berville

Destouches (1689) (Beauvais)
Michel Camus Destouches

Lostanges (1689) (Tulle)
Jacques Blanchet de Pierre-Buffiere

Montendre (1689) (d'Angouleme)
N. de Montendre

Cabanac (1689) (Languedoc)
N. de Cabanac

Milly (1689) (Lyonnais)
N. de Milly

Mirabeau (1689) (Provence)
N. de Mirabeau

Galiottes (1689)
Jean Martin
Three companies of Sailor/Marines formed to man the French flotilla on the Rhine. Martin actually became colonel in 1693 when the companies were first formed together.

Lorges (1689)
Guy Alphonse de Durfort, Comte de Lorges

Perigueux (1690)
Louis de Bouchet de Sourches Comte de Montsoreau
1692 Francois de Brigueville Marquis de Luzane
1693 Francois-Louis d'Hautefort Comte de Marqueyssac

Bressey (1692)
Jean-Claude de Belfrey Comte de Bressey

Albigeois (1692)
Jerome-Francois Lecuyer Comte de Muret

Thierach (1692)
Louis de Regnier Marquis de Guerchy

Laonnais (1692)
Jean-Louis de Cugnac Chevalier du Bourdet

Charolais (1692)
Gabriel d'Hautefort Chevalier de Montignac
1696 Bartlelemy-Gabriel Comte d'Espinay

Labour or Labord (1692)
Antoine de la Vore Marquis de Tourouvre

Bugey (1692)
N. Marquis de la Chaize
1695 Hyacinthe de Monvalet, Comte d'Entragues

Orleanois (1693)
Rene Marquis de Mailly

Oleron (1693)
N. le Veneur, Chevalier de Tillieres

Contentin (1693)
Jean-Louis de Wassinghac Chevalier D'Imécourt

Vosges (1693)
N. de Vandray Comte d'Autrey

Resnel (1695)
Louis de Clermont d'Amboise, Marquis de Resnel

Villefort
Louis-Francois d'Isarn Comte de Villefort

Bellaffaire
Joseph du Guast de Bellaffaire

Talende
Antoine de Pons Cher de Talende

Pons
N. Chev de Pons

de Laistre
N. de Laistre

Hautefort
Jean-Louis Comte de Hautefort

Du Biez
Antoine Oudant Marquis du Biez de Savignies Trecesson
Gilles de Came Marquis de Trecesson

Sourches
Louis-Francois de Bouchet Comte de Sourches

Monchy
Jean-Char de Bournel de Namps. Marquis de Monchy

Courbe
N. de Courbe

La Mothe
Clement de Guillard Comte de la Mothe

Sanzay (became Sourches)
Turpin de Crisse Comte de Sanzay

Vidame d'Amiens
Louis d'Albert D'Ailley Vidame d'Amiens
Lesparre
Leon de Madaillan de Lesparre, Marquis de Lassay

Vallouze
Joseph-Guillaume Bouten Comte de Vallouze

Soisy
N. de Soisy Langede
N. de Langede

Montjoue
N. de Montjoue

Beuzeville
N. de Beuzeville

Enonville
Pierre-Rene de Brisay, Comte d'Enonville

Dunchaux
N. De Dunchaux

Bioc
N. de Bioc Vavennes-Gourney
Joseph Alexandre de Nagu Marquis de Vavennes-Gournay

Stainville
N. de Choiseul Comte de Stainville

Bueil
Honorat Comte de Bueil-Racan

Choisinet
Franc de la Tour du Pu Comte de Choisinet

La Lande
N. du Deffant de la Lande

Beaurepaire
N. de Beaurepaire

Permangle
Gabriel de Chouly de Permangle

Siougeat
Jean de Layser Marquis de Siougeat

Bellefouriere
N. de Soyecourt Marquis de Bellefouriere

Barville
Andrew-Jules Comte de Barville

Marillac
Jean-Francois Marquis de Marillac
1696 Robert de Bouex de Villemort

Montalais
N. de Montalais

Conflans-Menars
Jean-Baptise Chairon, Marquis de Conflans-Menars

Brienne
N. de Loisiene de Brienne

Puynormand
Hardouin de Gauffretain de Puynormand

Hossifaire
N. de Hossifaire

Maisoncelles
Guillaume Texiede Maisoncelles

Servile
Guillaume de Massol de Servile

Courville
Francois Arnauld de Courville

L'Aigles
Jac-Louis d'Acres Marquis de L'Aigles

Lomagne
Gilles-Gervais de la Roche

Sezanne
Louis-Francois d'Harcourt Comte de Sezanne

Damas
Gilbert Comte de Damas, Chevalier de Damas
Jacques, Chevalier de Damas

Gallard
N. de Gallard de Beane

Pezaux
Cleriadus de Pra-Balesseau, Chevalier de Pezaux

La Force
N. de Caumont de la Force

Morignane
Paul Covet Comte de Marignane

Fus de Carrion-Nisas
H. Marquis de Carrion-Nisas

Artaignan
Pierre de Montesquiou Comte de Artaignan

Fusiliers

In August of 1695 six regiments of fusiliers were formed. I have no idea of their organisation, dress or flags but I suspect that like the earlier regiment of 'Fusiliers du Roi' (which will be covered with the artillery) these regiments served without pikes. This seems particularly likely given that none saw any action in the field but were used to garrison border fortresses (de La Croix; frontier at Luxembourg, de Guiscard: in Flanders, de La Bretesche: in Hainault, de Tesse; in Dauphine, de La Fare; in Nice and de Ximenes; on the Meuse).

I have sought to simplify the illustrations by not depicting the colonel's colour for every regiment. Only those regiments whose colonel's colour is not a white cross on a white field have therefore been shown.

The central illustrations on Plate 34 represent a reconstruction of two infantry drummers. The drummer of the Bourbon regiment wears the livery of the Dukes of Bourbon, in this case Monsieur, brother of the King. The livery is traditionally described as 'Ventre-de-biche' with 'Cramoisi' (creamy buff and crimson) lace. Interpretations of this vary from brown and deep maroon to orange and red. The same livery was worn by the regiment Conde, (a junior line of the house of Bourbon) but for some reason contemporary Frency experts seem to depict Bourbon musicians in the orange/red option whilst Conde musicians are shown in a light brown/deep crimson. On this occasion I have shown the liveries the same, but readers should be aware of possibilities for differencing them in their model armies. The other drummer is from the Languedoc regiment and wears the *Livree du Roi*. The position of the lace has been taken from a Lucien Rousselot plate depicting troops of the early eighteenth century, but given the tradition of drummers' lace during the seventeenth century seems a likely style for the 1690s.

The three figures on Plate 35 are derived from a Eugene Leliepvre plate in La Sabretache. They depicted three soldiers of the *Gardes Françaises* and were drawn using Giffart's 1696 illustrations as the primary source. I have removed the *Garde* insignia, trusting that the cut of the clothing and the equipment would be common to a line infantryman. I have left the bunches of shoulder lace, but whilst Rene Chartrand says that Languedoc wore dark yellow and red lace I have no knowledge as to whether Vermandois wore lace or what colour it might be.

The Regiments

LA SARRE
Mestres de Camp:
    1685 Francois-Albert, Marquis de Braque
    1691 Jean-Charles, Comte de Vaudray
Drummers: *Livree du Roi*

LA FERE
Mestres de Camp:
    1680 Rene-Armand de Mottier, Marquis de la Fayette
    1694 Francois de la Matte, Chevalier de Gennes

Drummers: *Livree du Roi*

ROYAL ROUSSILLON
Mestre de Camp:
    1672 Joseph, Comte de Ximenes
Drummers: *Livree du Roi*
One of the few 'French' regiments still wearing a colour other than grey. They adopted grey with blue facings in the next century.

CONDE
Mestres de Camp:
    1688 Nicolas, Comte de Montmorency
    1696 Marc, Chevalier de Montmorency
Drummers: Bourbon livery

BOURBON
Mestres de Camp:
    1684 Nicholas le Breton, Marquis de Villandry
    1690 Nicolas, Marquis de Vieuxpont
    1690 Guillame-Alexandre, Marquis de Vieuxpont
Drummers: Bourbon livery

BEAUVOISIS
Mestres de Camp:
    1685 Louis de Mienne, Marquis de Vieuzbourg
    1695 Nicolas d'Aix, Marquis de la Chaise
Drummers: *Livree du Roi*

ROUERQUE
Mestres de Camp:
    1678 Guy de Bourbon, Marquis de Maleuze
    1692 Phillippe de Beaufort, Marquis de Canillac
Drummers: *Livree du Roi*

BOURGOGNE
Mestres de Camp:
    1680 Francois-Joseph Bourton, Comte de Chamilly
    1697 Thomas de Breze, Marquis de Dreux
Drummers: *Livree du Roi*

ROYAL MARINE
Mestres de Camp:
    1676 Louis Fauste de Brichanteau, Marquis de Nantis
    1690 Louis-Armand de Brichanteau, Marquis de Nantis
Drummers: *Livree du Roi*

VERMANDOIS
Mestres de Camp:

1689 Nicolas de Bellefortiere, Marquis de Soyecourt
1690 Armand de Bethune, Marquis de Charost
1696 Antoine de la Vove, Marquis de Tourouvre
Drummers: *Livree du Roi*

LANGUEDOC
Mestres de Camp:
    1689 Antoine-Louis de Gondrin, Marquis d'Antin
    1696 Jean-Francois, Marquis de Marillac
Drummers: *Livree du Roi*

PLESSIS-BELLIERE/MONTSORREAU
Mestres de Camp:
    1675 Henri de Rouge. Marquis de PlessisBelliere
    1692 Louis de Sourches, Comte de Montsorreau
Drummers: unknown
Colours for Montsorreau (taken from Charrie)

JARZE/MONTENDRE/MEDOC
Mestres de Camp:
    1685 Marie-Urbaine du Plessis, Marquis de Jarze
    1691 Isaac de la Rochefoucaud, Comte de Montendre
Drummers: after 1692 *Livree du Roi*
Colours for Medoc (Charrie)
The regiment took the name of the province of Medoc in 1692

CLERAMBAUT
Mestre de Camp:
    1679 Phillippe de Palluau, Marquis de Clerambaut
Drummers: unknown
Colours as for Gensac (1702); may have been carried earlier

CASTRIES/MORANGIES
Mestres de Camp:
    1674 Joseph de la Croix, Marquis de Castries
    1695 Charles de la Molette, Marquis de Morangies
Drummers: unknown
Colours for Morangies. The border may be in smaller sections, the text (from Charrie) is not very detailed.

ROYAL COMTOIS
Mestres de Camp:
    1685 Louis Gigault, Marquis de Bellemond
    1692 Jean-Francois du Fay, Marquis de Vergetot
Drummers: *Livree du Roi*

MAULEVRIER
Mestres de Camp:

1689 Jules-Armand Colbert, Marquis de Blainville
1690 Nicolas Colbert, Marquis de Maulevrier
1695 Henri Colbert, Chevalier de Maulevrier
Drummers: unknown

PROVENCE
Mestres de Camp:
1684 Nicolas Lengle, Marquis du Magny
1689 Paul de Montmorency, Comte de Luxe
1693 Charles de Montmorency, Chevalier de Luxembourg
Drummers: *Livree du Roi*
Sergeants wore red coats etc. Regiment wore grey with red facings after 1702.

BOULONNAIS
Mestre de Camp:
1684 Henri Hurault, Marquis de Vibraye
Drummers: *Livree du Roi*

TOULOUSE
Mestres de Camp:
1684 Louis d'Hautefort, Marquis de Surville
1693 Jean, Comte de Cadrieu
Drummers: *Livree du Roi*

ANGOUMOIS
Mestres de Camp:
1685 Antoine de Longecombe, Marquis de Thouy
1690 Nicolas Dulac
Drummers: *Livree du Roi*

PERIGORD
Mestres de Camp:
1684 Louis d'Ornaison, Comte de Chamarande
1693 Jean de Barbezieres, Comte de Chemerault
1697 Henri, Marquis de Lambert de Saint Bris
Drummers: *Livree du Roi*

SAINTONGE
Mestres de Camp:
1684 Francois le Camus, Marquis de Bligny
Drummers: *Livree du Roi*

FOIX
Mestres de Camp:
1689 Nicolas de Bethune-Sully, Prince d'Henrichmont
1696 Joseph de Mesmes, Marquis de Ravignan
Drummers: *Livree du Roi*

Part 5: Foreign Troops in French Service

This section will cover the foreign troops which made up such an important part of the French army.

Organisation

With the exception of the Swiss the foreign regiments adopted the same battalion organisation as the rest of the French army. The Swiss formed larger battalions of 800 men in four large companies (compared to 690 men in 13 companies, the norm elsewhere). Note: The Swiss seemed to have, in general, preferred a small number of large companies per battalion as the same organisation was used by the Swiss in Dutch service.

The foreign regiments had the following numbers of battalions (from Susane's *Histoire de L'Infanterie Francaise*):

German regiments: Alsace 3 (4 after 1696), Greder (Allemand) 2, De Surbeck/ La Marck 2, Leisler/Sparre 2, Yoel/Royal Danois 2, Bernold 1

Swiss regiments: Erlach/Manuel 2, Stuppa (the elder) 4, De Salis/Porlier/ Reynold 2, Pfyffer/Hessy 4, Greder (Suisse) 2, Stuppa (the younger)/Surbeck 4, De Salis (the younger) 4, De Courten 2, Monnin 2, Oberkann/Porlier/ Schellemberg 2

Walloon regiments: Zurlauban 2. Famechoriasenghien 1, Boufflers/Mirornesnil 2, Soire 2, Robecque 2, Poitiers 2, Bouillon 2

Italian regiments: Royal Italien 1, St. Laurent/Nice 2, Thouy 2, Montroux 2. Casal 2. Montferrat 2, Savoie 2. Corsican regiment: Perri 2

Equipment and Dress

In general foreign regiments were equipped and dressed as the rest of the army. The only exception to this was (again) the Swiss. Pikemen in the Swiss regiments appear to have retained their helmets long after the practice of wearing protective headgear had been abandoned elsewhere.[1] Certain later reconstructions also show Swiss pikemen with tassets[2] and multi-coloured striped pikes.

GERMAN REGIMENTS

ALSACE (1656)
Marechal-de-Camp:
    1667 Chretien II de Baviere, Prince de Birkenfeld
    1696 Chretien III de Baviere, Prince de Birkenfeld

---

1   Pikemen wearing hats may well have been equipped with a protective iron scull-cap or 'secrete', such as was often supplied to cavalry.

2   Tassets are pieces of armour attached to the bottom of the breastplate which protect the thighs.

Drummers: *Livree du Roi*
Another member of the family was a Dutch lieutenant-general throughout the period.

GREDER ALLEMAND (1670)
Marechal-de-Camp:
   1686 Francois Laurent von Greder of Solothurn
Drummers: Coat as soldier, decorated with white lace. The flags depicted are, according to Charrie's *Drapeaux et Etandard du Roi*, correct for this period. By the time of the Battle of Blenheim, where two colours were lost, the top colour illustrated, the colonel's colour, had been replaced by one of similar style but with a crown head instead of the fleur-de-lys. Later still the regiment was probably issued with colours similar in type: those of Surbeck/La Marek (see illustration) but with red, white and blue chevrons decorating the outside of the regimental colour, instead of the red, white and yellow of Surbeck/La Marck. Although the regiment was considered to be German, the colonel was Swiss.

DE SURBECK/LA MARCK (or MARK) (1680)
Marechal-de-Camp:
   1680 Jean-Jacques de Surbeck
   1693 Ferdinand-Maxirnillian de la Marck, Comte de Furstenberg
   1697 Louis-Pierre, Comte de la Marck
Drummers: unknown.
The flags illustrated show the colonel's colour (top) for Surbeck and the regimental colour for Le Marck. The regimental colour for Surbeck would have the same central device with a white border of the style carried by the Montroux or Perri regiments.
   The colonel's colour of La Marck had the motto 'NEC PLURIBUS IMPAR' on a blue ribbon at the top with the globe, shown centrally positioned on the Surbeck colour, moved to the bottom. In between a 'Sun in splendour' device as depicted on the Zurlauban colonel's colour. The field remained white with a 'seine' of fleur-de-lys. Surbeck was also Swiss.

LEISLER/SPARRE (1690)
Marechal-de-Camp:
   1690 Jean Leisler
   1694 Erik-Magnus Taffeta, Baron Sparre
Drummers: yellow coats, white lace with blue-green spots. Regiments formed from men captured at Fleurus (1690) the soldiers were Germans serving in Swedish units hired by Holland. The first colonel in the regiment, Leisler, was a captain serving in the Swiss regiment of Stuppa the younger and was killed at Hostelrich (1694).

YOEL/ROYAL DANOIS (1690)
Disbanded 1698
Marechal-de-Camp:
   1690 Francois Yoel
   1692 Comte de Guldenlew

Drummers: unknown.
The regiment was formed from detachments from La Marck and Zurlauban, as well as some new recruits. The Comte de Guldenlew was an illegitimate son of the King of Denmark.

BERNOLD (1692)
Became part of **ALSACE** 1696
Marechal-de-Camp:
    1690 Sigefroi de Bernold
Drummers: unknown.
Formed from the Alsace militia

TOUL
A regiment listed by Rene Chartrand. I can find no details anywhere, apart from coat colours.

SWISS REGIMENTS

ERLACH/MANUEL (1672)
Marechal-de-Camp:
    1672 Jean-Jacques, Comte d'Erlach
    1694 Albert Manuel
Drummers: unknown. Fleur-de-lys on the colonel's colour were gold.

STUPPA (the elder) (1672)
Marechal-de-Camp:
    1672 Pierre Stuppa
Drummers: unknown.
Flags: unknown.

DE SALIS/PORLIER/REYNOLD (1672)
Marechal-de-Camp:
    1672 Jean-Rodolphe de Salis-Ziziers
    1690 Jean Porlier (or Pollier)
    1692 Francois de Reynold
Drummers: unknown.
Uniforms: Salis; red and green, Porlier; blue & red, Reynold; red & yellow. Porlier was colonel, for a short while, of another regiment (see below). This uniform could therefore apply to that unit also. The flag depicted is also for the regiment Porlier and the same could apply here.

PFYFFER/HESSY (1672)
Marechal-de-Camp:
    1672 Francois Pfyffer de Wyher
    1689 Gabriel Hessy
Drummers: unknown.
Uniforms: Pfyffer: yellow and red, Hessy: blue and red.

Flag: for Hessy the colours had five flames in blue, yellow, white, blue yellow.

GREDER (SUISSE) (1673)
Marechal-de-Camp:
    1673 Wolfgang Greder
    1691 Louis Greder
Drummers: unknown.
Flags: these colours were captured during the War of the Spanish Succession.
Wolfgang Greder died in 1691 from wounds suffered in 1690 at Fleurus.

STUPPA (the younger)/SURBECK (1677)
Marechal-de-Camp:
    1677 Jean-Baptiste Stuppa
    1692 Jean-Jacques de Surbeck
Drummers: unknown
Surbeck was previously colonel of a German regiment (see above).

DE SALIS (the younger) (1690)
Marechal-de-Camp:
    1690 Jean-Baptiste, Chevalier de Salis Soglio
Drummers: unknown
Uniform and flag depicted are for Regiment May.
Hans-Rudolf yon May succeeded Salis as colonel in 1702. Details for May might not be applicable to Salis. Regiment May is sometimes shown in a white vest.

COURTEN (1690)
Marechal-de-Camp:
    1690 Jean-Etienne de Courten
Drummers: unknown

MONNIN (1690)
Bcame part of De Courten in 1698
Marechal-de-Camp:
    1690 Francois Monnin de Neufchatel
Drummers: unknown

OBERKANN/POLIER (or PORLIER)/SCHELLEMBERG (1690), d.1698
Marechal-de-Camp:
    1690 Henri Oberkann of Zurich
    1690 Jean Polier of Lausanne
    1690 Jacques de Schellemberg
Drummers: unknown
Flag: as Porlier above

I do not know why it had three colonels within a year. As discussed earlier, the Porlier uniform could be blue and red. Although it seems unlikely that he would have time to introduce new uniforms, unless the Oberkann colonelcy had introduced those colours and the green and red was started by Schellemberg.

WALLOON REGIMENTS

ZURLAUBAN (1673)
Marechal-de-Camp:

    1685 Beatus Jacques de la Tour Chatillon, Comte de Zurlauban

Drummers: Light green coat with white lace.

Flag: Wagner (*Bemalungsangaben fur die Zeit des Spanischen Erbfolge krieges 1701–14*) shows the 'NEC PLURIBUS IMPAR' motto above the sun device on the colonel's colour and also a different regimental or ordinance colour, i.e. a white cross, quarter one light blue, two and three white, for light green.

Zurlauban was a brigadier during the Nine Years' War, and was promoted lieutenant-general in time for the Spanish Succession conflict. At the Battle of Blenheim (1704) Zurlauban was killed and his regiment suffered so badly that it had to be broken up.

FAMECHON/ISENGHIEN (1677)
Marechal-de-Camp:

    1677 Ignace de Belvalet, Comte de Famechon

    1697 Louis de Gand-Vilain de Merode de Montmorency, Prince D'Isenghien

Drummers: unknown

Flags: Charrie lists two alternative sources for the colours of Isenghien (Famechon's colours are unknown) without judgement. Thus both are included.

BOUFFLERS/MIROMESNIL (1688)
Disbanded in 1714
Marechal-de-Camp:

    1688 Francois, Duc de Boufflers

    1690 Nicolas, Comte de Boufflers

    1694 Jean-Baptiste Hue, Marquis de Miromesnil

Drummers: The 1706–11 Bouffler Regiment's drummers wore green coats with red cuffs and lining. The coat was decorated with gold and white lace, the white lace had alternate red crosses and rose heads.

The same regiment had flags of the following pattern, which were captured at Malplaquet (1709): white cross, each quarter three straight edged flames, red, white, green. With a white border decorated with eight red rose heads and eight crosses. This flag is a possible alternative to the red and green bars which cannot be confirmed as the correct colour. The yellow and black colour was carried during the period in which Miromesnil was commanding. Interestingly the red and green bars flag was certainly carried by the 1721–7 Boufflers regiment, ironically this regiment was, during the 1690s, regiment Solre, details of which are listed below.

SOLRE (1688)
Marechal-de-Camp:
  1688 Ferdinand-Francois de Croi, Comte de Solre
Drummers: unknown

ROBECQUE (1688)
Marechal-de-Camp:
  1688 Phillippe-Marie de Montmorency, Prince de Robecque
  1691 Charles de Montmorency, Prince de Robecque
Drummers: unknown

POITIER (1688)
Disbanded in 1714
Marechal-de-Camp:
  1688 Frederic-Leonor, Comte de Poitiers
Drummers: unknown
Flag: the standard shown is that of the regiment Croi-Solre. The Chevalier Croi-Solre having become colonel in 1700. No details are known on the dress of the regiment.

BOUILLON (1688)
Marechal-de-Camp: 1688 Nicolas Tour d'Auvergne, Duc de Bouillon
Uniforms, flags, drummers: unknown

ITALIAN REGIMENTS

ROYAL ITALIEN (1671)
Marechal-de-Camp: 1671 Bardo dei Bardi, Comte Magalotti
Drummers: *Livree du Roi*
Magalotti was a Captain in the *Gardes Françaises*, when the newly formed regiment paraded before the King he was so impressed he gave them the 'Royal' title. The brown coats were worn well into the eighteenth century.

ST. LAURENT/NICE (1678)
Marechal-de-Camp:
  1678 Jean-Baptiste de Ferraro, Marquis de St. Laurent
  1691 Le Comte de Nice
Drummers: as Nice, may have been treated as a provincial regiment and worn the *Livree du Roi*. At the time of the regiment's formation Nice was part of the territory of Victor Amadeus II, Duke of Piedmont-Savoy and was therefore treated as a foreign regiment, not attaining French provincial status until the eighteenth century.

MONTFERRAT (1688)
Disbanded in 1706
Marechal-de-Camp: 1688 Nicolas, Marquis de Natte
Drummers: unknown

From 1690 the regiment was given the title Royal Montferrat and after 1702 *Gardes* du duc de Mantue. Like St. Laurent the original troops were Piedmontese. No details of uniforms.

SAVOIE (1688)
No details of the Marechal-de-Camp. The regiment served in garrisons in Flanders and was disbanded in 1698. No detail of dress, flags etc.

THOUY (1690)
Marechal-de-Camp:
   1690 Antoine-Balthazar de Longcombe, Marquis de Thouy
Drummers, uniforms: unknown
Formed from Piedmontese prisoners captured in 1689

MONTROUX (1690)
Marechal-de-Camp:
   1690 Phillippe-Marie de Montroux
Drummers: unknown
Formed in the same way as Thouy and disbanded in 1715

CASAL (1692)
Marechal-de-Camp:
   1692 Pierre de Perrien, Marquis de Crenant
Uniforms, flags, drummers: unknown
Garrison of Casal, disbanded in 1695

ST. SEGOND (1693)
Marechal-de-Camp:
   1693 Francois de Rossi de Baville, Marquis de St. Segond
Uniforms, drummers: unknown.

THE CORSICANS

PERRI (or PERT) (1690)
Disbanded in 1715
Marechal-de-Camp:
   1690 Jean-Baptiste, Marquis Perris de Genes
Drummers: unknown

5

The French Army in the War of the Spanish Succession

Part One

The regiments in this section were all raised before or during the War of the Grand Alliance. After a short section on some of the changes in equipment and dress which affected French troops during the Spanish Succession War, there follows a list of the regiments showing any changes in uniforms or colonels.

Equipment and Dress

Between 1689 and 1714 fashionable male attire would consist of the following:

The Hat

In 1689 this would normally be felt or beaver with a large brim and a low crown. The size of the brim was beginning to reduce after the excesses of the 1670s. The edge of the brim was often decorated in gold or silver lace, and feathers and ribbon were added for further decoration. The ribbons however were now less obtrusive than previously and were often worn in an embryonic form of cockade. In the 1660s and 1670s hats had been worn in a multitude of colours, grey and brown being particularly popular, however by the middle of the last decade of the century black was the dominant colour. During the 20-year period following 1689 there was also a gradual move towards tricorns. It is difficult to quantify how this came about or how fast it occured, but by the end of the first decade of the eighteenth century the tricorn was firmly established as the pre-eminent form of headgear. One of the biggest problems in determining the process of change is the difficulty of accurately dating primary visual sources. For example there are a great number of paintings and other forms of illustration depicting Louis XIV heroically conducting sieges, at the theatre or playing billiards, but very few can be dated closely to the event they depict. The evidence seems to point to a fairly rapid adoption of the tricorn between 1698 and 1702, but these dates are really only guesses based on the following observations:

Illustrations of Louis XIV which can be dated to between 1692 and 1695 show no particular tricorn-type hats amongst the King and his courtiers.

The works of Gifford and Guerard, which date from the end of the War of the Grand Alliance, show a mixture of styles, with Gifford showing most officers in tricorns and the men in other types and Guerard depicting tricorns of a particular 'loose' style being worn by all.

The problem is compounded at the other end of our historical period as most pictures of Marlborough, Eugene etc. date from well after the original events. The tapestries should be reasonably correct, given that the man himself helped in their design, but the works of Laguerre and Ross date from later and should not be too heavily relied upon. Ironically Ross's paintings of Marlborough's campaigns show hats turned up on one or more sides, but no tricorns. Whether he was attempting to portray his concept of the dress of 1704–9 or whether he was working from 'eyewitness' accounts is unknown. Despite this degree of uncertainty it seems likely that both officers and men in the majority of European armies had by the middle years of the War of the Spanish Succession adopted some form of tricorn hat.

Small Clothes

Amongst the fashionable many changes had been wrought during this period, however as only the neckwear is particularly relevant to the men and their officers I will confine my comments to this area.

The 'beau' of 1689 would have worn a lacy 'rabat' or 'raban' (a neck scarf) wrapped around and decorated with ribbons. The ribbons were stiffened and positioned behind the raban to protrude either side in a sort of 'halo' effect. In 1692 the French won the closely fought battle of Steenkirk and the folklore arising from the battle changed the direction of French costume. The soldiers of the French army had been surprised in camp by the army of William III and had to hurriedly dress and equip themselves. In their haste they are supposed to have left their neckcloths untied and their clothes in a disorderly manner. This gave rise to the 'Steenkirk'style of wearing the raban and a general adoption of more 'relaxed' forms of dress. The Steenkirk was loosely wrapped around the neck and the longer end pulled through the seventh buttonhole on the coat. By the end of the century a more formal style had been re-established, but without the ribbons. The ends of the cloth were now more often tucked in and this led to the rank and file using a reversed form as shown on the plates. You will see from the plates that the neckcloths are shown as being black, the Wagner plates show this for all infantry and whilst I have some doubts about the widespread use I have, in the absence of much contradictory evidence, used black for my illustrations.

The Coat and Vest

During the period the coat or *justacorps* became more obviously styled. The straight, shapeless item of the 1680s had by the last years of the century gained rear pleats and a more well-defined silhouette. The coat sleeves became longer and wider and the sleeves of the vest or waistcoat could no longer be seen. The vest itself, which had as late as 1698 been as long as the coat, became noticeably shorter as the eighteenth century proceeded.

Shoes and Stockings

No major changes are apparent here, the shoes became 'heavier' and shorter, in the process losing some of their elegance, but were still square toed and the red heels generally fashionable from the middle of the century were still retained by the Dutch amongst others.

Wigs

Finally, in passing, a few changes were taking place in the design of periwigs. As the period progressed they continued the process of looking less like natural hair which had begun in the late 1660s. They became taller with, from the mid 1690s, considerable peaks discernable at their summits. The colours too became less natural, with grey and white becoming popular after the century had turned.

Weapons and Equipment

The French infantry that emerged to begin the conflicts of 1701 had changed somewhat from the 'fantassins' of 1697. Firstly, the musketeer who had retired into winter quarters for the last time after the Treaty of Ryswick had become a fusilier. By 1702 the re-equipping of the French army with flintlock muskets or fusils had been almost completed. They had not, however, adopted the platoon methods of fire control used by their Dutch, English, and German enemies. In the earlier wars the Grand Alliance had been so out-generalled that the advantages of their superior tactical doctrine had not been appreciated, but this time it would be different. Also missing from the French infantry battalion, and likewise from most other European armies, was the pikeman. The introduction of the flintlock together with the socket bayonet, which enabled fire to continue even when the bayonet was fixed, had sounded the death knell for the 'queen of battles'. Also contributing to the demise of the pike were the new tactics. Linear formations three to five ranks deep were trained to deliver massed volleys, and without the offensive polearms of before the firepower of the battalion became the method of deciding infantry engagements. So critical is the change in tactics that modern historians seem to be of the opinion that with the exception of the disputing of built-up areas and fortifications, the infantry vs infantry melee all but ceased to exist.

To go with the fusil a new set of equipment was issued to the French soldier. The cartouche box was now a smaller 'belly' pouch attached to the waist belt, the shoulder belt was thinner and only held up the powder flask. The sword was still attached to the waist belt, but the bayonet, which had previously hung alongside the cartouche box on the right hip, was now positioned with the sword.

The Regiments

Below are listed all regiments formed before 1701 which were still in existence on that date. Part Two of this chapter will detail those units formed during or after 1701.

Any changes in colonels are shown and the colour plates show all alterations in the uniforms or flags of these units. Unless stated otherwise, units not illustrated retained the same colours in their uniforms, but cut to the new style (see the earlier parts of this series for details of these). Likewise where the commanding officer of 1697 is still in command during the War of the Spanish Succession his details will be listed under the regiment in the earlier part. Tables showing the war records of the regiments are also shown below

PICARDIE
1702: Pierre-Armand de Rohan, Prince de Montbazon

CHAMPAGNE
1702: Marie-Jean-Baptiste Colbert, Marquis de Seignelay
1712: Rene-Francois de Froulay, Chevalier de Tease

PIEMONT
Christian-Louis de Montmorency, Chevalier de Luxembourg
1705: Anne-Jacques, Chevalier de Bullion
1711: Louis-Antoine-Armand de Gramont, Duc de Louvigny

NAVARRE
1706: Gilbert de Chabannes, Marquis de Pionsae
1709: Jean, Marquis de Gassion

NORMANDIE
1709: Anne-Auguste de Montmorency, Comte d'Esterre
1713: Pierre-Charles Regnauld, Comte d'Ange nes

LEUVILLE
1700: Louis-Thomas du Bois de Fiennes, Marquis de Leuville

BOURBONNAIS
1700: Louis de Brichanteau, Marquis de Nangis
1709: Louis-Antoine de Gramrnont, Comte de Le-sparre

AUVERGNE
1703: Jean-Louis de Wassinghac, Chevalier d'Imecourt
1705: David d'Alba

SAULT/TESSE/TALLARD
1703: René-Mans de Froulay, Comte de Tessé
1707: Marie-Joseph de Hostun, Duc de Tallard
Flag in Plate 38 is that of Regiment Tallard

NETTANCOURT/MAILLY/BUEIL-RACAN/BROSSE/BOUFFLERS-RAMIANCORT
1704: Adrien de Silly, Comte de Mailly La Houssaye
1708: Antoine-Pierre, Comte de Bueil-Racan
1712: Francois-Henri de Thiercelin, Marquis de Brosse
1713: Charles-Francois, Marquis de Boufflers-Ramiancort
Drummers of Nettancourt as per Plate 38. Illustration in plate shows dress of

Mailly with inset of officer's cuff.
Flags: top, Mailly; bottom, Brosse

ARTOIS
1703: Claude-Guillame Testu, Marquis de Balincoun
POITOU
1702: Louis-Charles de Montsaulnin, Marquis de Montal

LYONNAIS (no change)

CRUSSOL/d'ANTIN/GONDRIN/GERVAISAIS
1702: Antoine-Louis de Pardailian-Gondrin, Marquis d'Antin 1703: Louis de Pardailian, Marquis de Gondrin
1712: Auguste-Nicolas de la Gervaisais
Plate 38 shows flag for Gondrin

TOURAINE
1703: Jean-Baptiste-Francois Desmarets, Comte de Maillebois

ANJOU
1710: Louis de Conflans, Marquis Armentieres

MAINE
1700: Nicolas, Marquis de Saguiran
1703: Francois-Arnauld de Courville
1707: Alexandre de Dammartin, Marquis de Belrieux

On the death of Turenne the regiment was given to the Our de Maine, the bastard son of Louis XIV. Although the dress of the regiment stayed the same, new flags were issued. These were: quarters 114 yellow, 213 crimson.

HUMIERES/CHAROST/BETHUNE/SAILLANT
1702: Louis-Joseph de Bethune. Marquis de Charost
1709: Michel-Francois, Chevalier de Bethune
1712: Charles-Francois de Estaing, Marquis de Saillant
The flag in Plate 38 is that of Saillant

COETOUEN/TOURVILLE/MEUSE
1709: Jean-Baptiste-Cesar de Costentin, Marquis de Tourville
1712: Henri-Louis de Choiseul, Marquis de Meuse
Illustration shows the uniform worn throughout the period
Top flag: CoetquencTourfille, bottom; Meuse

GRANCEY/LA CHESNELAYE
1707: Adolpe-Charles de Rominey, Marquis de la Chesnelaye
Flag and dress for both regiments as per Plate 38

LA RUNE
1702: Nicolas d'Omaison, Marquis de Buxancois
1706: Louis-Pierre-Maximillian de Sully, Duc de Bethune
1711: Daniel-Francois de Gel as de Voisins de Lautree, Chevalier d'Ambres

LA MARINE
1702: Pierre Le Guerchois de St. Columbe
1709: Michel Chamillard, Marquis de Cans

LIMOUSIN
1703: Nicolas du Bois, Marquis de Givry
1706: Nicolas Leon Phelippes de la Houssaye

ROYAL DE VAISSEAUX
1702: Isaac-Charles de Rochefoucauld, Comte de Montendre
1702: Louis de Regnier, Marquis de Guerchy
1705: Thomas Le Gendre de Collendre

ORLEANS
1706: Joseph de L'esquen, Marquis de la Villemeneust

LA COURONNE
1707: Rene-Francois de Froday, Chevalier de Tesse
1712: Jean-Baptiste, Comte de Polastron

ROYAL
1703: Pierre-Rene de Brissay, Comte d'Enonville
1705: Louis-Francois, Comte d'Aubigne de Tigny

BRETAGNE
1704: Michel-Francois Bertheiot de Rebourseau

PERCHE
1705: Nicolas Cotteron
1706: Claude, Marquis de Ceberet

ST. SULPICE/LANNOY/DE LOUVIGNIES
1702: Nicolas de Crussol d'Uxes, Comte de St. Sulpice
1708: Louis-Auguste, Comte de Lannoy
1712: Jean-Maignsirt de Bernieres de Louvignies
Dress worn throughout
Flags for St. Sulpice/Lannoy and Louvignies

VENDOME/DUC DE BERRY/BARROIS
None of the above name changes were due to a change in field commander
but were gifts from the King. The colonel lieutenant changes just once during
the period; see below.
1712: Rene-Jean-Baptiste de Coskaer d'Ablois, Marquis de Vieuville

After the Regiment Barrois was given to the Duc de Conti (see below) this regiment then became the new regiment of the province Barrois.

LA SARRE
1704: Nicolas Fabry, Comte de Moncault
1709: Henri Fabry de Moncault, Comte d'Autrey

LA FERE
1703: Nicolas, Comte Desmarms
1704: Louis Desmoulins, Marquis de Lisle

ALSACE (German; no change)

ROYAL ROUSSILLON
1701: Nicolas de Ximenes, Marquis de Proissy
1708: Augustin, Marquis de Ximenes

CONDE
1710: Phillippe-Claude de Beaufon, Marquis de Momboissier
1712: Pierre-Charles Regnault, Comte d'Angennes
1713: Nicolas de Haute fort, Comte de Surville

LE ROI
1706: Louis de Prevost. Marquis de B arai I
1711: Louis de Brichanteau, Marquis de Nangis

DAUPHIN
1704: Jean-Baptiste de Rochcchouan, Comte de Maure
1710: Louis de Clermont-Tonneure. Marquis de Chastes

BOURBON
1704: Nicolas, Comte de Vieupont
1704: Guy-Claude-Roland, Comte de Laval-Montmorency

BEAUVOISIS
1705: Nicolas de Revol
1707: Pierre-Maximillian de Pajot de Villeperot

ROUERGUE
1704: Nicolas de Rigollei
1706: Louis-Athanase de Puechpeyrou de Comminges

BOURGOGNE
1704: Nicolas de Rigollet
1701: Joachim-Adolpe de Sieglieres de Boisfranc, Marquis de Soyecourt

ROYAL MARINE
1709: Louis Desmarets de Maillebois, Baron de Châteauneuf

VERMANDOIS
1706: Nicolas de Vove, Chevalier de Tourouvre
1709: Francois-Lazare Thomassin, Marquis de St. Paul

GREDER ALLEMAGNE (German; no change)

ROYAL ITALIEN
1705: Francois-Zénobe-Philippe, Marquis Albergotti

LANGUEDOC
1704: Pierre d'Arros, Baron d'Argelos
1712: Jean-Armand, Comte d'Argelos

REYNOLD/CASTELLAS
1702: Francois-Nicolas-Albert de Castellas
Was de Sallis/Porlier
Plate 39 shows details of Regiment Castellas

VILLARS-CHANDIEU
1701: Charles de Villars-Chandieu
Was Erlach/Manuel, see Plate 38

BRENDLE
1701: Jost Brendle
Was Stuppa, see Plate 38

MONTSERREAU/VANDREUIL/SOURCHES
1704: Nicolas de Rigaud, Marquis de Vaudreuil
1706: Louis-Francois du Bouchet, Comte de Sourches

TOULOUSE
1703: Jean-Louis, Comte de Hautefon-Bosen

BOULONNAIS
1703: Louis-Alexandre Verjus, Marquis de Crecy

ANGOUMOIS
1702: Nicolas de Rouge, Marquis de Plessis-Belliere
1707: Hardouin de Gaufreteau de Puynormand
1710: Nicolas de Coetartcourt

PEPJGORD
1711: Nicolas de Boisset de Geaix
1714: Nicolas de Briqueville, Marquis de La Luzeme

SAINTONGE
1705: Anne Bretagne, Marquis de Lannion

FOIX
1709: Pierre de Thome

OUERCY
1705: Jean-Sebastien Hue, Chevalier de Miromesnil

FOREZ
1704: Jean-Baptiste, Comte de Polastron
1712: Etienne-Joseph d'Isarn, Marquis de Villefort

CAMBRESIS
1702: Francois-Louis Hautefort, Comte de Marqueyssac
1708: Jerome-Auguste de Boisset, Marquis d'Arville

TOURNAISIS
1705: Jean-Francois de Biaudos, Marquis de Casteja

NIVERNAIS
1701: Nicolas de Montmorency-Luxembourg
1704: Paul-Hippolyte Sanguin, Chevalier de Livry

GUYENNE
1713: Eberhard-Ernest, Comte d'Harling

LORRAINE
1703: Jean-Charles de Boumel de Namps, Marquis de Monchy
1710: Comte de Mothe-Houdancourt
1711: Jean Etienne de Varennes-Goumay
It is probable that the regiment wore green cuffs during the period of the War of the Grand Alliance.

FLANDRE
1702: Thomas le Gendre de Collandre
1705: Francois-Armand dc Laurencin, Marquis de Mison

BERRY
1704: Auguste-Nicolas-Magon, Marquis de la Gervaisis
1712: Nicolas Magon de la Gervaisis, Comte de la Giclaye

BEARN
1702: Jean-Baptiste de Rochechouart, Comte de Maure
1704: Paul-Auguste-Gaston de La Rochefoucauld, Comte de Montendre et de Jarnac

HAINAUT (no change)

BIGORRE
1702: Nicolas de Scull

1709: Gabriel-Jacques de Salignac, Marquis de Fenelon

BRESSE
1706: Francois, Marquis de Mommorency-La-Neuville

LA MARCHE
1702: Alexandre-Thomas du Bois de Fiennes, Bann de Givry

BRIE
1709: Nicolas de Raffetot

SOISSONAIS
1705: Andre-Jules, Comte de Barville

ISLE-DE-FRANCE
1710: Nicolas de Buraulure

VEXIN
1703: Jacques Barbier du Metz d'Espinay

AUNIS
1704: Charles Hugues, Comte de Lyonne
1710: Henri-Antoine-Thomas, Chevalier de Brancas-Courbon

BEAUCE
1703: Nicolas Du Repaire
1708: Joseph Pierre Dejean de Manville

DAUPHINE
1704: Nicolas de Kercado-Molac
1706: Jean-Baptiste de Vassal, Comte de Montviel

VIVARAIS
1705: Rene-Augustin d'Erard, Chevalier de Ray

LUXEMBOURG (no change)

BASSIGNY
1702: Anne-Jacques, Chevalier de Bullion
1705: Jean-Francois, Marquis de Creil-Nancre

ZURLAUBAN (Walloon; no change)
Regiment destroyed at Blenheim, colonel killed
Disbanded

BEAUJOLAIS
1702: Nicolas de Menestral de Hauguel de Luteaux
1704: Etienne de Nenestral de Hauguel de Luteaux

PONTHIEU
1707: Jean-Hector de Fay, Marquis de la Tour-Maubourg

SILLERY/CHATELET-LOMOND
1701: Felix-Francois Bruslart, Marquis de Sillery
1707: Florent-Claude, Marquis du Chatelet
Plate 39 depicts the dress and flag for Sillery

SOLRE/BEAUFORT (Walloon)
1709: Nicolas, Chevalier de Croi-Solre (brother of previous commander)
1709: Albert-Francois de Croi, Comte de Beaufort
Flag in Plate 39 for Beaufort

MIROMESNIL (Walloon; no change)

ROBECQUEST, VALLIER (Walloon)
1704: Nicolas de la Croix, Chevalier de St. Vanier
1714: Henri-Bernard de la Croix, Chevalier de St. Vanier

CROI-SOLRE/AUNAY
1700: Alben-Francois, Chevalier de Croi-Solre
1709: Jean-Charles de Mesgrigny, Comte d'Aunay

GARDES DU DUC DE MANTOUE (Piedmontese)
1700: Francois-Zenobe-Philippe, Comte Albergotti
1702: Prosper de Gonzague, Marquis de Luzzara
1704: Nicolas de Jaucoun de La Valserie
Until 1702 the regiment was known as Montferrat and then Royal Montferrat.

TESSE/SANZAY
1703: Lancelot de Turpin de Crisse, Comte de Sanzay
Flag for Tesse, see Plate 39 for Sanzay details
Dress remained the same
Galiotes (sailors; no change)
No uniform details. Seem to have carried a black flag like Piemont

SPARRE/LENCK (German)
1714: Jacques-Gustave de Lenck
MAY (Swiss)
1702: Jean-Rudolphe May
Illustrated in Plate 39. Some minor changes in dress from Salis the Younger

COURTEN (Swiss; no change)

LEE (Irish; no change)

CLARE/O'BRIEN (Irish)
1706: Morgan, Comte O'Brien

DILLON (Irish; no change)

THOUY (Piedmontese; no change)
Disbanded 1706

MONTREUX (Italian; no change)

PERRI (Corsican; no change)

NOAILLES/BEAUFERME/BRICHAMBAULT
1704: Nicolas de Beaufermes
1708: Joseph-Perrin de Brichambault
No change in uniforms or flags during this period

CHARTRES
1709: Philippe-Charles, Marquis d'Etampes

BLAISOIS
1703: Nicolas de Ferrieres, Marquis de Sauveboeuf

GATTNAIS
1704: Philippe-Charles, Marquis de La Fare

BARROIS/CONTI
1704: Jean-Jacques Desmoulins, Chevalier de Lisle
1710: Charles-Francois, Marquis de Bouffler-Ramiancourt
1713: Louis-Anne-Francois de la Rochefoucauld, Comte de Marthon-Roucy.
This was a provincial regiment given to the Duc de Conti in 1714. The illustration in Plate 38 shows the dress and flag of the regiment before 1714.

AUXERROIS
1702: Nicolas d'Amfreville
1709: Louis-Henri d'Harcoun, Comte de Beuvron

AGENOIS
1705: Henri-Louis de Choiseul, Marquis de Meuse
1712: Nicolas, Chevalier de Broglie

SANTERRE
1704: Nicolas de Cetseans
1708: Michel-Jean-Baptiste Charron, Marquis de Conflans-Menars

THIERACHE
1702: Henri, Marquis de Carrion-Nisas

ALBIGEOIS
1710: Nicolas du Deffand de La Lande

LAONNAIS
1710: Ferdinand-Agathange, Marquis de Brun

CHAROLAIS
1712: Jacques Berbier du Metz

LABOUR
1710: Claude-Alexandre, Comte de Bonneval
1706: Georges de Raymond

BUGEY
1701: Pierre, Comte de Beranger

LES LANDES
1704: Alexandre-Maximilien-Balthazar-Dominique de Grind d'Isenghien. Comte de Middelbourg

ORLEANNAIS
1700: Nicolas, Marquis de La Boulaye
1711: Marie-Joseph de Brancas, Marquis d'Oyse

OLERON
1707: Jean de Leyser, Marquis de Siogeat

COTENTIN
1703: Michel-Camus Destouches
1711: Nicolas, Marquis de Chabannes

VOSGES
1704: Jacques-Antoine de Ricouard, Marquis d'Herouville

ST. SECOND (Italian; no change)

DORRINGTON (Irish; no change)

BERWICK (Irish; no change)

BOURKE/WAUCHOPE (Irish)
1715: Francis Wauchope

ALBEMARLE/FITZGERALD/O'DONNELL (Irish)
1703: Nicholas Fitzgerald
1708: Daniel O'Donnell

GALMOY (Irish; no change)

Part Two

The regiments listed here and in Part Three were formed or reformed during or after 1701. With the exception of two, Royal Baviere and Enghien (see Part Three) all were disbanded at the end of the war, if not before. With the exception of the few foreign regiments raised, all carried plain colonel's colours. The drapeau d'ordinance, where known, are listed. Little information is available on the uniforms of these regiments, but for those of you who wish to be able to use the flag details and reconstruct the regiments, the evidence seems to show that they were more likely to wear red than blue cuffs on their grey coats.

OURCHES/BOULAY/EPPEVILLE
1702: N. Comte de Ourches
1705 N. du Boulay
1710: Francois de Bovelles d'Eppeville
Service: Italy

LOUVIGNIES/SIFFREDY
1702: Jean-Meignard de Bernieres de Louvignies
1712: N. de Siffrecly
Service: Flanders, Oudenarde and Malplaquet

TAVANNES
1702: Charles-Henri Gaspard de Saube, Vicomte de Tavannes
Service: Blenheim

MARCILLY
Reformed in 1701 for an earlier regiment.
Service: Chiari and Turin.

DESTOUCHES/MONTMORENCY/de MASSELIN
Reformed (as above)
1700: Francois de Montmorency-La Neuville
1706: Jean-Claude de Masselirt

LOSTANGE/RASILLY
Reformed (as above)
1707: N. de Rasilly
Service: Ramillies

GALIOTTES
Reformed (as above)
Boat troops for service on the waterways. Flag identical to Piemont.

BELL AFFAIRE/TESSE/BULKELEY/BOCHET
Reformed (as above)
1705: Rene Francois de Froulay, Chevalier de Tesse
1707: Francois Comte de Bulkeley

1709: N. du Bochet
Service: Almanza

TALENDE/DUCHAY/d'ARCY
Reformed (as above)
1705: N. Duchay
1709: N. d'Arcy
Service: Flanders

DU BIEDFLAMARENS
Reformed (as above)
1710: N. de Grossoles de Flamarens
Service: Ramillies and Oudenarde

TRECESSON
Reformed (as above)
Service: Rhine

LA MOTHE/d'ARTAIGNAN
Reformed (as above)
1709: Louis de Montesquiou, Comte d'Artaignan
Service: Blenheim, Ramillies, Oudenarde and Malplaquet

SANZAY/SOURCHES/CHOISEUL-BEAUPRE
Reformed (as above)
1703: N. du Bochet, Chevalier de Sourches
1706: Antoine Baron de Choiseul-Beaupre
Service: Flanders

LASSAY/LA MOTHE
Reformed (as above)
1710: N. Marquis de la Mothe d'Hugues
Service: Landau. Speyerbach, Blenheim and Denain

VALLOUZE/GROSSBOIS/VALENCE
Reformed (as above)
1704: N. Grossbois
1708: Emmery Emmanuel de Thimbrune Marquis de Valence

ENONVILLE/LIVRY/BELZUNCE
Reformed (as above)
1703: Paul Hippolyte Sanguin, Chevalier de Livry
1704: Charles-Gabriel de Castelmoron Chevalier de Belzunce
Service: Landau, Speyerbach, Blenheim and Denain

VARENNES-GOURNAY/d'ENTRAOUES
Reformed (as above)
1703: Victor de Montvalet Marquis d'Entraques

Service: Ramillies

CHOISINET/CORDES/VILLENEUVE/CAYLUS
Reformed (as above)
1705: N. de Cordes
1710: N. de Villeneuve
1712: Henri-Joseph, Comte de Caylus-Rouairoux
Service: Italy

PERMANGLE/MAULMONT
Reformed (as above)
1708: N. de Maulmont
Service: Lille

SIOUGEAT
Reformed (as above)
Service: Turin

VILLEMONT
Reformed (as above)
Service: Lille

CONFLANS-MENARS/d'ASTOUR/d'HERNOTON
Reformed (as above)
1708: N. d'Astour
1711: N. d'Hemoton
Service: Flanders, Moselle, Rhine and Oudenarde

L'AIGLE
Reformed (as above)
Service: Flanders garrisons

CHEVALIER DE DAMASNALLOUZE
Reformed (as above)
1708: Joseph-Guillame Boutin, Comte de Valloue
Service: Turin

PEZAUX/de la EERIE
Reformed (as above)
1702: N. de la Fors de la Ferte
Service: Landau and Lille

MARIGNANE/SERVILLE/BEAUJEU
Reformed (as above)
1705: Guillame de Massol de Serville
1709: N. Comte de Beaujeu
Service: Italy

FOURGEUVAUX/SOURCHES
1702: Jean-Baptiste de Pavie Baron de Fourgeuvaux
1703: Louis Francois de Bouchet Comte de Sourches
Service: Flanders and Ramillies (regiment destroyed, colonel seriously wounded)

GASSION
1702: Jean Chevalier de Gassion
Service: Italy, Turin, Flanders and Oudenarde

MONTBOISSIER/LONGUERUE
1702: Philippe-Claude Marquis de Montboissier-Beaufort
1710: N. de Longuerue
Service: Blenheim

LA LONDE/FRANCLIEU/BOUGIS
1702: N. Chevalier de la Londe
1706: N. de Franclieu
1710: N. d Bougis

ST. GERMAIN-BEAUPRE
1702: Armand-Louis-Joseph Foucauld, Chevalier de St. Germain-Beaupre
Service: Flanders

LA CRU/CARAMAN/LANNON
1702: N. de la Cm
1705: N. Riquetti de Caraman
1711: Anne Bretagne, Marquis de Lannion
Service: garrisons

BROGLIE/FROULAY/TIRAQUEAU
1702: Victor-Maurice Comte de Broglie
1703: N. Chevalier de Froulay
1711: N. Tiraqueau
Service: Italy, Turin and Flanders

BRANCAS/LABADIE
1702: N. de Brancas
1709: Marie-Joseph de Brancas, Marquis de Oyse
1711: N. de Labadie
Service: Flanders

ST. AULAIRE/CHATEAUBRIANT/MONTVIEL
1702: N. de St. Aulaire
1706: Louis Desmarets de Maillebois, Baron de Chateaubriant
1709: Jacques Vassal, Marquis de Montviel
Service: Flanders, Malplaquet and Denain

ROZE/PROVENCHERES/USSY
1702: N. de Roze de Rosen
1704: N. de Provencheres
1706: Pierre-Jean de Carcary d'Ussy
Service: Rhine

NUAILLE
1702: Charles Germain le Mast in Comte de Nuaille
Service: Flanders and Oudenarde

GUITAUD/CHAMAILLES
1702: Louis-Athanase de Puechpeyrou de Comminges Comte de Guitaud
1706: Louis-Guillame-Victor Comte de Marloup de Chamaifles
Service: Rhine and Alps

VILLENOUVET/LA FONS/DE MATHA
1702: N. de Villenouvet
1706: N. de is Fans
1710: N. de Bourdeilles Comte de Matha
Service: Moselle

DESCLOS/NUPEES/LESPINAY
1702: N. Desclos
1705: N. de Nupces or Nupees
1711: N. de Lespinay
Service: Italy and Alps

TURBILLY
1702: Louis-Philippe de Menou Marquis de Turbilly
Service: Flanders, Moselle and Rhine

LA FARE
1702: Charles-Auguste, Comte de la Fare-Soustelle
Service: Turin and Denain

VIVOURS/BRIOUZE/VASIERES
1702: N. de Vivours
1705: N. de Briouze
1712: N. des Vasieres
Service: Rhine and Alps

DES FEUGERETS/VAUVRAY/BARBANCON
1702: N. des Geugerez or Feugerets
1706: Alexandre-Lopuis de Girardin de Vauvray
1707: Francois du Prat de Nantouillet, Comte de Barbancon
Service: Flanders garrisons

SILLY/MAILLE
1702: N. de Vipart de Silly
1705: N. Comte de Maille or Mailly
Service: Rhine. Blenheim and Flanders garrisons

RICHEBOURG/BARVILLE/RIBERAC
1702: N. de Richebourg
1704: Andre-Gules Comte de Barville
1710: N. de Riberac
Service: Flanders and Alps

BLACONS
1702: Armand Vicomte de Blacons
Service: garrisons

TARNAULT/BOISSIEUX
1702: N. de Tamault
1707: Louis de Fretat, Comte de Boissieux
Service: Rhine

LANNION
1702: Anne-Bretagne Marquis de Lannion
1705: Jean-Baptiste Pierre, Chevalier de Lannion
Service: guarding the Brittany coastline

MENOU
1702: Charles Marquis de Menou de Cuissy
1706: Louis Joseph Comte de Menou
Service: Cassano and Turin (colonel lost a leg)

TOURNON/PAYSSAC
1702: Louis du Pasquier de Toumon
1709: Francois Dunaes Comte de Payssac
Service: Italy and Spain

LA MOTHE/GHISTELLES/PERTHUIS
1702: N. de la Mothe-Houdancourt
1709: N. de Ghistelles
1712: N. de Perthuis
Service: Flanders garrisons

GENSAC/PIFFONEL
1702: N. de Gensac
1703: Gilles-Gervais de la Roche-Lomagne Marquis de Gensac
1711: N. de Pilfonel
Service: Landau and Speyerbach (colonel killed)

ST. EVREMONT
1702: Charles de St. Evremont
Service: Flanders garrisons

GUINES/DAMPIERRE
1702: N. de Guines
1705: Jacques-Joseph Huet de Dampierre
Service: Flanders

CHALMAZEL
1702: Louis de Talaru. Marquis de Chalmazel
Service: Rhine

CASTEJA/ST. LEGER
1702: Jean-Francois de Biaudos, Marquis de Casteja
1705: Charles-Louis, Comte de Casteja
1709: N. de St. Leger
Service: Flanders garrisons

COETANFAU/Du ROURE
1702: N. de Coetanfau
1706: Ange Urban de Beauvoir-Grimoard, Comte du Roure
Service: garrisons

POYANNE
1702: N. Marquis de Poyanne
Service: garrisons

SAVIGNY/BOISSET/BERARD
1702: N. de Savigny
1708: N. Boisset de Geaix
1711:N. Berard
Service: Rhine and Landau

FRANCHEVILLE/ROCHEFORT/BEAUFICEL
1702: N. de Francheville
1709: N. de Gassaut de Rochefort
1712: N. de Beauficel

BROISSIA/FONTANGES
1702: N. de Broissia
1708: N. de Marquis de Fontanges
Service: Rhine and Flanders

MAISONTHIERS
1702: Charles de Tussaut de Maisonthiers
Service: Alsace garrisons

PUJOI/PUYSEGUR/LEOTAUD/VALORY
1702: N. de Pujol
1706: N. de Puysegur
1708: N. de Leotaud
1712: Guy-Louis-Henri, Marquis de Valory
Service: Flanders

DIOGNY/DU THIL
1702: N. de Diogny
1704: Francois-Edouard Juben Marquis du Thil
Service: Lille

CARNE/HOCCART
1702: N. de Came
1708: Zacharie Hoccart

HEROUVILLE/THESUT/CONFLANS ST. REMY
1702: N. de Herouville
1704: N. de Thesut
1710: Alexandre-Philippe Chevalier de Conflans St. Remy
Service: Flanders

DESMARETS/VERSIELLES
1702: N. Desmarets
1708: N. de Versielles
Service: Flanders

CAUPOS
1702: N. de Caupos
Service: Flanders

CLERMONT/DE LA HOUSSAYE/VASSAN
1702: N. de Clermont
1705: Nicolas-Leon Phillipes de la Houssaye
1706: Charles, Marquis de Vassan

PFYFFER (SUISSE)
1702: Louis Pfyffer de Wyher
Service: Ramillies, Oudenarde, Lille and Denain
Uniform: possibly yellow coats and red cuffs etc.

VIGIER (SUISSE)
1702: N. Vigier de Steinbruck de Soleure
1708: N. Tiester
Service: Flanders

ARTAIGNAN
Reformed (as above)
1704: Pierre-Paul de Montesquiou Comte d'Artaignan
Service: Ramillies and Denain

MONTENDRE/BERTHELOT/d'ESGR1GNY
1701: Paul-Auguste Gaston de la Rochefaucauld Comte de Montendre
1702: Michel Francois Berthelot de Rebourseau
1704: Jean-Rene le Jouenne d'Esgrigny
Service: Chivasso, Cremona and Turin

MONTPEYROUX/MONTAROIS/CHATILLON
1701: N. de Oregon i des Gardies, Marquis de Montpeyroux
1702: N. d Montarois
1704: N. de Chatillon
Service: Italy (regiment was captured at Pianezza in 1706)

BOUZOLS/LA/FORCE/LASSAY
1701: N. Marquis de Bouzols
1705: N. Marquis de Caumont de la Force
1711: N. de Madaillan de Lesparre Chevalier de Lassay
Service: Italy

DURFORT-BOISS1ERES
1702: N. de Durfort-Boissieres
1703: Saturnin Marquis de Durfort-Boissieres
Service: Cassano and Turin

La FAILLE (Walloon)
1702: N. de la Faille
Service: Flanders (disbanded in 1709)

BRYAS/CROUBOURNONVILLE (Walloon)
1702: N. Comte de Bryas
1703: N. Prince de Croi
1704: N. Chevalier de Bournonville
Service: Flanders, Speyerbach

BANDEVILLE
1702: N. Marquis de Bandeville
Service: Blenheim (colonel killed, regiment disbanded)
CHABRILLANT
1702: N. de Moreton Marquis de Chabrillant
Service: Blenheim (colonel killed, regiment disbanded)
Uniform (not illustrated): grey coat, red cuffs, vest, breeches & stockings.
Yellow buttons, hat lace. Drummer: red coat with grey cuffs. No details of lace.

ALBARET
1702: N. Chevalier d'Albaret
Service: Blenheim (colonel killed, regiment disbanded)

SANGUIN/COURNIERES
Reformed (as above)
1702: N. de Cournieres
Service: Rhine and Flanders

LA TOUR MAUBOURG/THOMASSIN ST. PAUL
1702: Jean-Hector de Fay Marquis de la Tour Maubourg
1707: Francois Lazare Thomassin de St. Paul
Service: Flanders and Moselle

LANNOY
1702: Louis-Auguste, Comte de Lannoy
Service: Rhine and Spain

MARTEULAUBANIE
1702: N, de Mattel
1710: N. Rousseau de Laubanie

ROUSILLES
1702: Louis-Theodore d'Escorailles de Fontanges Marquis de Rousilles
Service: Rhine garrisons

MONTFORTARVILLE/du PRAT/du SOUPA
1702: N. de Montfort
1706: Jerome-Augustin de Boisset Marquis d'Arville
1708: N. de Prat
1710: N. de Soupa
Service: Flanders

LA GUISE/MONTESSON
1702: N. de la Guise
1706: Charles, Comte de Moniesson
Service: Rhine and Alps

FROULAY/LE TORIERES
1702: Charles-Francopis. Comte de Froulay
1711: N. Chevalier de Letorieres
Service: Flanders

ST. SIMON/VOLUIRE/ANGENNES/VARENNES-KERGOSON
1702: N. Chevalier de St. Simon
1705: Philippe-Auguste. Comte de Voluire
1708: N. d'Angennes
1711: Francois. Chevalier de Varennes-Kergoson

LAVAL/SENNECTERRE
1702: Guy-Claude Roland de Montmorency, Comte de Laval
1705: Jean-Charles de la Ferte Marquis de Sennecterre
Service: Flanders and Bouchin

CASTELET
1702: Charles-Felix Hyacinths de Galean des Issants, Marquis de Castelet
Service: Rhine garrisons

BERWICK ETRANGER
1702: James Fitzjames Duke of Berwick
1704: O'Berghiez
1708: O'Davan
Formed from British Army deserters. Served in Flanders.

ROSIERES/CHEVRON/BONNIERES
1702: N. de Rosieres
1707: N. de Chevron
1712: N. de Bonnieres
Service: Flanders

LA ROCHE DU MAINE/DESANGLES
1702: N. de la Roche du Maine
1707: Georges de Renard Desangles
Service: garrison

MONTLUC/LA RIVIERE-CASTERAS
1702: Francois de Lasseran-Massencome Marquis de Montluc
1707: Pierre de la Riviere-Casteras
Service: Italy

DESPREZ/ROHAN
1702: Jean-Baptiste Thibault de la Rochethulon Desprez
1710: N. Chevalier de Rohan

BORNEMONT/BEAUJEU
1702: N. de Boniemont
1709: N. Comte de Beaujeu
Service: Flanders

PERTHUIS/MOROOUES/DU BOURG
1702: N. de Perthuis
1708: N. de Moroques
1712: N. de Bourg
Service: Rhine

BROSSES/ORMOY
1702: N. de Brosses

1711: N. d'Ormoy
Service: garrisons

REDING ALLEMAND
1705: Jean-Francois, Chevalier de Reding de Biberegg
1706: Gilles-Gervais de la Roche-Lomagne
1707: Baron de Reding
Service: Italy. Spain and Almanza. Flag shown is one of two possible designs. The other is illustrated elsewhere

SCEVE/CHOISEUL/MURAT
1702: N. Chevalier de Sceve
1702: N. Choiseul-Stainville
1703: N. Choiseul-Meuse
1703: N. Choiseul-Francieres
1705: N. de Murat
Service: Rhine, Friedlingen, Landau and Speyerbach (colonel badly wounded)

Part Three

This section covers more regiments formed between 1701 and 1709. All apart from Royal Baviere were disbanded at the end of the conflict. Royal Baviere was formed from the old Bavarian army almost destroyed after Blenheim and the remnants of which were now exiled, along with their sovereign, in Flanders.

LA RAIMBAUDIERE
1702: Alexandre de Goyon, Marquis de la Raimbaudiere
Service: garrisons

BOUFFLERS-REMIANCOURT/CHOISEUL
1702: Charles Francois, Marquis de Boufflers-Remiancourt
1710: N. Chevalier de Choiseul
Service: Flanders, Lille and Malplaquet
Drummers may have dressed in green as Boufflers

PISANCON/LESOUEN DE VILLEMENEUST
1702: N. de Pisancon
1707: N. de Lesquen de Villemeneust
Service: Italy and the Alps

AUBIGNE/NOGARET
1702: Louis-Francois, Comte d'Aubigne de Tigny
1705: Francois de Calvisson, Marquis de Nogaret
Service: Flanders

VAUDREUIL/BRANCAS/LOSTANGES
1702: N. de Vaudreuil

1706: Henri-Antoine-Thomas, Chevalier de Brancas-Courdon
1710: N. Marquis de Lostanges-Beduer
Service: Flanders

ARGINY/AUBUSSON/VARENNES-GOURNAY
1702: Antoine Camus, Comte d'Arginy
1706: N. d'Aubusson
1708: Jean-Baptiste de Varennes-Gournay
Service: garrisons

LACHAU-MONTAUBAN
1702: Francois-Hector de la Tour du Pin, Comte de Lathan-Montauban
Service: Rhine and Flanders

LA FEUILLADE
1704: Louis d'Aubusson, due de la Feuillade
Service: Italy and Turin

TESSE (Savoy)
1704: Rene de Froulay, Comte de Tesse
Service: Alps

MONTENEGRE (Piedmontais)
1704: Jean-Baptiste, Marquis de Montenegre (disbanded in 1705)

BELTRAMBI (Italian)
1705: N. de Beltrambi (disbanded in 1706)

RANGONI (Italian)
1705: N. de Rangoni (formed from the Milicia of Modena)

FUSILIERS DE MONTAGNES — 4 battalions
1705: Bonaventure d'Orffa de Villeplana (from the Roussillon Milicia)
Service: Pyrenees

SEGUR/DANOIS
1705: N. de Segur
1706: Henri-Francois, Comte de Segur
1709: Louis-Francois de Gernay, C*Comte* de Danois
Service: Spain (Villaviciosa)

NOE
1706: Marc Roger, Marquis de Noe
Service: Roussilion and Spain

THORIGNY/CHAMBAUD
1706: N. de Thorigny
1706: N. de Chambaud (two battalions formed from the Milicia of Caen)

Service: Flanders

JAUCOURT/MANCINUCHASTES/CLERMONT-MONTOISON
1706: N. de Jaucourt
1708: N. de Mancini
1709: Louis de Clermont-Tonnerre, Marquis de Chastes
1710: N. de Clermont-Montoison

DUC DE NOAILLES/LA BAUME
1706: Adrien-Maurice, due de Noailles
1713: N. de la Baume
Service: Roussillon

MARECHAL DE NOAILLES/BOUHYER
1706: Anne-Jules, Marechal de Noailles
1709: Benigne de Bouhyer
Service: Roussillon and Dauphine

CHAMILLY/MORNAC
1706: Noel Bouton, Marechal de Chamilly
1707: Charles-Leon Boscal de Reals, Comte de Mornac
Service: garrisons

GRIGNAN/BELLAFFAIRE
1706: N. de Grignan
1707: Joseph du Guast de Bellaffaire
Service: Spain (Almanza)

BOUFFLERS/BOMBELLES
1706: Antoine-Charles Louis, Comte de Boufflers
1711: Henri-Francois, Comte de Bombelles
Service: Flanders (Oudenarde, Malplaquet, Denain)

VILLEQUIER/LE TELLIER/LA MOTE
1706: N. d'Aumont de Villequier
1709: N. Le Tellier
1712: N. de La Motte
Service: Flanders garrisons

CLAIRFONTAINE/TALLYRAND/MAULEVRIER
1706: N. de Clairfontaine
1712: N. de Tallyrand
1714: N. de Maulevrier
Service: Spain

ROMAINVAL/CORMIS
1706: N. de Romainval
1712: N. de Cormis

Service: Alps

CONFLANS/LAVAL/RUYS
1706: N. de Conflans
1709: N. Comte de Laval
1712: N. de Ruys
Service: Flanders garrisons

URBAN/AMBRES or UMBRES/GUIGNONVILLE
1706: N. d'Urban
1710: Daniel-Francois de Gelas de Voisins, Chevalier d'Ambres
1712: N. Lenain de Guignonville
Service: Flanders (defence of Quesnoy)

BRAGNY/VIELLEVIGNE/GRANDLIEU/ARROS/DES HAYES
1706: N. Chevalier de Bragny
1707: N. de Crux de Viellevigne
1708: N. de Crux de Grandlieu
1710: Jean-Armand, Comte d'Arros d'ArgeIos
1712: N. Des Hayes
Service: Flanders garrisons

CHOISEL/HOUDETOT
1706: N., Chevalier de Cholsel
1712: N., Chevalier d'Houdetot
Service: Spain

KAERGROET or KEROUARTZ/SEBBEVILLE
1706: N. de Kaergroet
1708: Francois Cadot, Chevalier de Sebbeville
Service: Flanders garrisons

LA LONDE
1706: N. Chevalier de la Londe
Service: garrisons

BRUSCART/GOELLO
1706: N. de Bruscart de Siliery
1712: N. de Goello
Service: garrisons in Alsace

BOURDONNE/CHAMPIGNY/CASTELNAU
1706: N. de Bourdonne
1707: N. de Champigny
1712: N. de Castelnau
Service: Spain and Dauphine

Comte d'HOUDETOT/CAYLUS
1706: N. Comte d'Houdetot
1712: N. Chevalier de Caylus
Service: Flanders garrisons

SAILLANT/USSEL
1706: Charles-Francois d'Estaing, Marquis de Saillant
1712: N. d'Ussel
Service: Dauphine and the Rhine

VILLELONGUE/MONTREAU
1706: N. de Villelongue
1710: N. de Montreau
Service: garrisons

BAUMELAY/MOUCHAN/DAMAS/HOUDETOT
1706: N. de Baumelay
1707: Jean de Castillon, Comte de Mouchan (killed at Tortese 1708)
1708: Jean-Jacques, Chevalier de Damns
1712: N. Comte d'Houdetot
1714: N. de Regnier, Comte de Guerchy
Service: Spain and Dauphine

GRAMMONT/SCEVE
1706: N. Marquis de Grammont
1709: N. Chevalier de Sceve
Service: Alps

MONTSORREAU
1706: Louis-Vincent du Bouchet de Sourches, Chevalier de Montsoreau
Service: garrisons

ABLOIS de la VIEUVILLE
1706: N. de Ablois de la Vieuville
Service: Dauphine

PONT du CHATEAU/LEON
1706: N. Marquis de Pont du Chateau
1710: N. de Roan, Chevalier de Leon
Service: Spain and Dauphine

PAYRELA/STORFF (Walloon)
1707: Col. N. Payrela
1710: Col. N. de Storff

PANTOKA/BYLANDT (Walloon)
1707: N. Pantoka
1709: N. Baron de Bylandt

Service: Flanders

WEINLEY/HAMAT (Walloon)
1707: N. de Weinley
1709: N. d'Hamat

RHEINGRAF/HOUDENHOE (German)
1707: N. de Rheingraf
1708: N. Baron d'Houdenhoe
Service: Flanders

NASSAU/TREFFERD/UHLAND (German)
1707: Comte de Nassau
1709: N. de Trefferd
1711: N. Uhland
Service: Flanders

ALBERGOTTI/LETTERIO (Italian)
1707: N. Albergotti
1711: N. Letterio
Service: Flanders

GRIMALDI/CAETANO (Italian)
1707: N. Grimaldi
1711: N. Caetano
Service: Flanders

LOS RIOS (Spanish: called Las Sierras after 1710 and Leon after 1711)
1707: Col. N. de Los Rios
Service: Flanders

MACHIENO/VILLESCA (Spanish)
1707: Col. N. Machieno
1711: N. de Villesca

SOHE/MIGNONS/KERKEM (Walloon)
1707: Col. N. de Sohe
1709: N. de Mignons
1711: N. Baron de Kerkem
Service: Flanders

ASSIGNY/SCEPEAUX
1707: N. de Cosse, Marquis d'Assigny
1708: N. de Beaupreau, Marquis de Scepeaux
Service: Flanders

CANILLAC/BELLESUVEE/FEUQUIERES
1707: N. de Canillac

1708: N. de Bellesuvee
1710: N. de Pas, Chevalier de Feuquieres
Service: Flanders

PRATAMANO/CARAFFA (Italian)
1707: Col. N. Pratamano
1711: N. Caraffa
Service: Flanders

EVOLY/BACHER/COUPIGNY (Walloon)
1707: Col. N. d'Evoly
1709: N. de Bacher
1710: N. de Coupigny
Service: Flanders

MATRIMONT/BOURE (Walloon)
1707: Col. N. de Matrimont
1710: N. de Boure
Service: Flanders

RUPPELMONDE/BOURNONVILLE (Walloon)
1707: Col. N. Marquis de Ruppelmonde
1711: N. Chevalier de Bournonville
Service: Flanders

POLEON (Walloon)
1707: N. de Poleon
Service: Flanders

ROYAL BAVIERE (German)
1707: Maximillian-Emmanuel of Bavaria (formed from two companies of the Bavarian Guards and six of the French Regiment d'Alsace)
Service: on the Rhine

The following regiments have flags details listed in Charrie, but I can find no information on their formation or history: Chateaubriant, St. Andre, St. Gery, Saulieu or Souillac.

Bibliography

Barthorp, Michael, *Marlborough's Army* (London: Osprey Publishing, 1980)

Carasso-Kok, M. & Levy van Helm, J. (ed.), *Schutters in Holland Zwolle/Haarlem* (Zwolle: Waanders, 1988)

Childs, John, *The British Army of William III* (Manchester: Manchester University Press, 1987)

Childs, John, *The Nine Years' War & the British Army 1688–97* (Manchester: Manchester University Press, 1991)

Condray, Pat A., *Wargamers Guide to the Age of Marlborough* (USA, 1988)

Grew, M.E., *William Bentinck & William III* (London: Murray, 1924)

Hamilton, E., *William's Mary* (London: Hamish Hamilton, 1972)

Haswell-Miller, A.E., & Dawnay, N.P., *Military Drawings and Paintings in the Royal Collection*, (London: Phaidon, 1966)

Joubert, P., *Nouveau Guide de L'Heraldique* (Rennes: Ouest-France, 1984)

Louda, Jiri & Maclagan, Michael, *Lines of Succession* (London: Time Warner Books, 1981)

Maguire, W.A., *Kings in Conflict* (Belfast: Blackstaff Press, 1990)

Ringoir, H., *De Nederlandse lnfanterie* (Bussum: Van Dishoeck, 1967)

Sapherson, C.A., *Dutch Army of William III* (Leeds: Raider Books, 1990)

Sapherson, C.A., *Marlburian Armies 1700–21* (Leeds: Raider Books, 1991)

Schulten, C.M. & Smits, E.J.H.Th., *Grenadiers en Jagers in Nederland* (s'Gravenhague: Staatsuitgeverij, 1980)

Tincey, John, *The British Army 1660–1704* (London: Osprey Publishing, 1994)